The MONOCLE
Travel Guide Series

Vienna

For more information, please visit *gestalten.com*

Bibliographic information published by the Deutsche Nationalbibliothek: The Deutsche Nationalbibliothek lists this publication in the Deutsche National-bibliografie; detailed bibliographic data are available online at *dnb.d-nb.de*

Monocle editor in chief: *Tyler Brûlé*
Monocle editor: *Andrew Tuck*
Books editor: *Joe Pickard*

Designed by *Monocle*
Proofreading by *Monocle*
Typeset in *Plantin & Helvetica*

Printed by *Offsetdruckerei Grammlich, Pliezhausen*

Made in Germany

Published by *Gestalten*, Berlin 2016
ISBN 978-3-89955-662-9

Welcome
—— Vienna,
a splendid city

Austria's capital is as grand as its imperial history. The stately streets at the centre of the former Habsburg empire are lined with palaces and *Baroque masterpieces* that recall a time when the monarchy ruled from within the walls of the Hofburg Palace and *Mozart, Schubert* and *Beethoven* drew crowds at the *Vienna State Opera*. Art nouveau gems, examples of Vienna's artistic *Secession movement* and contemporary landmarks – such as Austria's tallest tower by architect Dominique Perrault – change up the urban landscape of this city by the *Danube*.

The Unesco-listed 1st district is undoubtedly worth a visit but there's more to Vienna than its *gilded past* and swarming *St Stephen's Square*. The city has updated itself to suit its hard-earned title as one of Europe's prettiest and *most liveable cities* and there are few that are as easy to traverse. Its 23 districts are pedestrian- and bike-friendly and navigating on public transport is a cinch.

While each neighbourhood is singular, they all have one thing in common: an abundance of coffeehouses. These *storied cafés* act as public living rooms where one can sit, sip a *melange* coffee and peruse the papers. Or perhaps one of the city's *heuriger* wine taverns is more up your alley?

This guide will take you off the beaten track to the independent shops, *family-run restaurants* and cultural hotspots that you might otherwise miss (but we also find room for the buzzing *Museumsquartier* and Baroque Belvedere palaces to whet your appetite for *Klimt* and *Schiele*). Read on for our tour of vibrant Vienna. — (M)

Contents
── Navigating the city

Use the key below to help navigate the guide section by section.

H Hotels

F Food and drink

R Retail

T Things we'd buy

E Essays

C Culture

D Design and architecture

S Sport and fitness

W Walks

Culture
The city that great artists and composers from Gustav Klimt to Mozart have called home leads the way when it comes to the arts. See the best of the cultural assets with our guide to museums, galleries housing experimental and classic art, and historical cinemas.

Design and architecture
From Baroque edifices to brutalist constructions and contemporary spaces, this is the backstory to the city's aesthetic highlights.

Sport and fitness
Don't let a city break get in the way of your fitness regime. We've put the leg work into rounding up the best places in the city for breaking a sweat, be it in or on the water, along the tarmac or gliding on the powdery stuff in the mountains. Plus: the finest grooming emporiums to keep you looking the part.

Walks
One of the best ways to get to grips with a city is by hitting the streets. But where to start? We visit five of the city's most diverse and interesting neighbourhoods to highlight enlightening routes through the best that each has to offer.

Resources
Our expert advice for enjoying Vienna like a local, with the best events, transport tips and essential vocabulary. There's also a playlist to accompany your trip and suggestions for what to do on a rainy day.

About Monocle
Find out more about our global brand, from groundbreaking print, radio, online and film output through to our cafés and shops.

Acknowledgements
The people who put this guide together: writers, photographers, researchers and all the rest.

Map
—— The city at a glance

From the imperial grandeur of the central district to the Majolikahaus and Prater park, Vienna's well-known sights won't disappoint. But crowds also flock here for the neighbourhood atmosphere that comes from the city's structure: surrounding the Innere Stadt are 22 other districts, marked by waterways from the outlying Danube to the Donaukanal (Danube Canal), and the Wien River that runs through the heart of the city.

A surprising number of parks range from manicured and royal to delightfully natural and ungroomed, while the hills – which get steeper towards the outskirts – help to make Vienna one of the only capitals in the world with operational vineyards.

Keep your eyes peeled and you'll find culture in the strangest places, such as the waste incinerator with a façade created by artist Friedensreich Hundertwasser. And since Vienna is experiencing the fastest population growth in central Europe, things are only going to get better. Stay tuned.

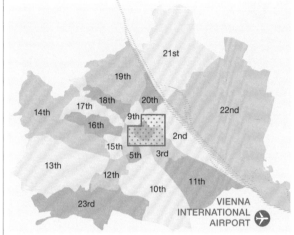

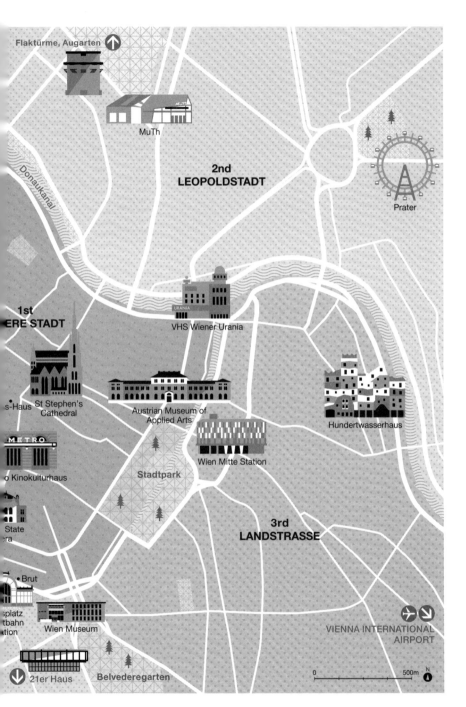

Flaktürme, Augarten

MuTh

**2nd
LEOPOLDSTADT**

Prater

VHS Wiener Urania

**1st
ERE STADT**

s-Haus St Stephen's
Cathedral

Austrian Museum of
Applied Arts

Hundertwasserhaus

METRO

o Kinokulturhaus

Stadtpark

Wien Mitte Station

**3rd
LANDSTRASSE**

State
era

• Brut

splatz
tbahn
tion

Wien Museum

VIENNA INTERNATIONAL
AIRPORT

21er Haus Belvederegarten

0   500m   N

Need to know
—— Get to grips
with the basics

The Viennese enjoy playing host but it helps to be an informed guest: one who can order coffee Viennese-style and knows the importance of a handshake. Read on for a few tips to make a first (or any) visit to the Austrian capital that little bit easier.

Districts by numbers
Neighbourhoods

Vienna's beating heart is the 1st district, Innere Stadt. Beyond the grand Ringstrasse, 22 other suburbs more or less wind around the centre. Across the Donaukanal (Danube Canal) is the large, traditionally Jewish 2nd district, which has recently become a trendy Brooklyn to the centre's Manhattan. Inner districts 3 to 10 are small and residential: the 6th and 7th skew bohemian, the 8th and 9th are a bit posher. Only outside the second ring, the *gürtel* (belt), do districts differ visibly: southern areas are working class, to the north are villas and vineyards. The Viennese identify with their districts. You'll know which one you're in by the street signs: the district number is listed before the street name.

Shopping hours
Retail

When it comes to shopping, Vienna's Catholic background becomes painfully obvious come Sunday morning. Nothing is open except for a few kiosks at the train station. So it's vitally important that you shop for sustenance or anything else you need before 19.00 on weekdays (some supermarkets stay open until 20.00) and on Saturdays, lest you go hungry on your day of rest. Other caveats: many retail outlets and smaller businesses close entirely in August, and Austrian national holidays have a way of sneaking up out of the blue on newbies or visitors (there are lots of Catholic ones not observed elsewhere). So keep an eye on the calendar and do some research before a big journey.

And guess what coffee is called over here – melange!

Social customs
Manners

Fail to introduce yourself, or forget the all-important handshake and you might get lost in Vienna's social shuffle or worse, be branded as a bit of a loser. Take the initiative among new people and offer your name and a firm and friendly handshake, even if it's not a business situation, and you'll fit right in. Ladies, Vienna gents open doors and look after coats. It's seen as chivalrous here (the older generation might kiss your hand; just go along with it, lips don't touch).

Glass half empty
Attitude

As charming as the Viennese can be, they also have a reputation for being incredibly grumpy (it's even a term: *wiener grant*). Despite living in one of the world's most consistently highest-ranked cities for quality of life, many have a talent for finding whatever's wrong with a given situation (or making up something that might possibly go wrong, or be better elsewhere). What to do? Just remind them how good they have it and offer another round of schnapps.

Pedestrian concerns
Getting about

Vienna gets more and more pedestrian-friendly; designated walkways as well as new bike paths are proliferating throughout the city but their markings can sometimes be confusing so watch your feet (and back). Austrian drivers are obliged to stop for pedestrians the second they step onto the street, which is reassuring – but don't push your luck. Stay within crosswalks and observe the city's new LGBT-friendly traffic lights (installed for Eurovision 2015) and you'll be fine.

Green idylls
Parks

The city's streets are narrow and its districts are often densely constructed but more than half of Vienna is green, with vast royal parks. The Volksgarten and Schönbrunn palace grounds can be overrun in tourist-heavy months such as August, so follow the Viennese to Augarten and Prater parks in the 2nd district, the Alte Donau waterfront parks on Donauinsel Island or Wienerwald forest area at the edge of town for idyllic hiking.

Vienna's parks are so popular, it can be hard to find a spare perch

Take your time
Etiquette

Slow down. This is not a city that likes quick business meetings, fast coffee breaks or one-hour dinners. The Viennese like to get to know who they're working with, extending the conversation and maybe talking culture or philosophy. Be sure to allow for a slower pace of life to happen here and not rush the getting-to-know-you phase or any phase thereafter, or you'll disturb the equilibrium and very possibly miss out on the best thing the city's people have to offer: their humour and hospitality.

I'm learning to embrace slow living

In vino veritas
Wien wines

This is the only capital city where wine is produced in significant quantities in vineyards within its limits. Best known are one-grape whites such as *grüner veltliner* but coming up fast in connoisseur circles are *gemischter satz*, a mixed-grape white, and the fruity red *blauer zweigelt*. The Viennese order their glasses by measure (ask for an *achtel* – an "eighth" of a litre) and enjoy drinking in inner-city wine bars or the *heurigen* (taverns) in the grounds of vineyards.

Coffee terminology
Culture

Viennese coffee culture is legend: asking for a latte usually doesn't cut it here so it's important to order Viennese-style. A *melange* (a version of a cappuccino) is the safest bet; a *kleiner* or *grosser brauner* (small or big "brown one") is steamed coffee served with a separate mini-pitcher of milk. A *mokka* is strong, short and black, a bit like espresso, and an *einspänner* is black coffee topped with whipped cream. Your coffee is always served on a tiny silver tray with a complimentary glass of water.

Don't take any brusqueness you may experience from your waiter personally; feel free to stay all day and pay homage to famous former café-dwellers such as Sigmund Freud, Gustav Klimt and Leon Trotsky.

Top tips
Payments

Tipping is common in Austria but people expect smaller amounts than in North America and some other parts of Europe. Servers are usually paid fairly and service charges are embedded in establishments' prices, so it's customary to simply round up a bit when paying the bill. A couple of euros to the next round sum if the bill is moderate, for larger bills about 5 to 10 per cent (maximum) is fine for good service.

It's important not to leave the tip on the table – it's considered an insult – and know that saying *Danke* when handing over the payment means "Keep the change". Tip about 10 per cent to taxi drivers and give a euro or two to porters in hotels.

Hotels
—— At home in Vienna

The Viennese do five-star stays in a grand manner that few cities can compete with but the time-tested swank and ceremony aren't all the Austrian capital has to offer. A clutch of sprightly independents has opened in recent years to challenge the more traditional options and created a diversity of dwellings that belie the city's diminutive size and conservative image.

From a townhouse in Neubau and a towering bank and converted shopfronts (now apartments) to a former brothel, new spaces are opening that are bolstering Vienna's hotel scene. Read on for our survey of the fluffiest pillows and bounciest beds in the Austrian capital.

①
Grand Ferdinand,
Innere Stadt (1st)
Elegant restraint

The stately Grand Ferdinand is a tasteful gear change from the team behind Hotel Daniel (*see opposite page*), who specialise in design-minded accommodation where the frills are optional. This hotel opened in October 2015 after a careful year-and-a-half refit of the 1950s building. As you enter, the first thing that greets you is a Viennese 18-candle crystal chandelier from glass specialist J & L Lobmeyr.

But this is where the stuffy ceremony ends. The reception and lobby are spare but homely – and patrolled by attentive staff. Hang left for a 200-seat restaurant dotted with wooden Thonet chairs, ruby-red leather booths and accents. Upstairs there are 188 well-appointed rooms – none carpeted, most spacious and simple – and up top there's a bright eighth-floor terrace (guests only, mind). It's perched on the southeastern stretch of the Ringstrasse so expect views to the city's east and north towards the twinkling Donaukanal. An attractive cocktail crowd forms come nightfall.
*10-12 Schubertring, 1010
+43 (0)1 91 880 400
grandferdinand.com*

MONOCLE COMMENT: The Viennese tend not to frequent hotels as they do restaurants or bars but the tall windows that showcase the hotel's inviting restaurant to the street outside may change this.

Wheely good time
——
Guests can hire one of the hotel's vehicles – choose from either a sporty Maserati Quattroporte or a 1964 Jaguar. The Jaguar once belonged to Dr Hans Lauda – grandfather of Austrian Formula One world champion Niki Lauda – whose company formerly occupied the building.

Once I finish this email I'm taking the Jag for a spin

High life
—
A guest-only roof terrace offers great views

②

Hotel Daniel, Landstrasse (3rd)
Contemporary class

Hotel Daniel is unerringly cool. Cue smart modern suites, a bakery serving honey produced on-site and apples from the garden, and hammocks in several of the 116 rooms.

The hotel is itself a landmark; it was built in 1962 by architect Georg Lippert, who also created the Daniel's sibling hotel in Graz (a happy coincidence only discovered by owner Florian Weitzer after the purchase).

The magnificent Belvedere Museum and its Gustav Klimt collection is within strolling distance, as is the 21er Haus with its contemporary exhibitions. If you prefer wheel-powered transport, the hotel has bicycles and Vespas for hire.
5 Landstrasser Gürtel, 1030
+43 (0)1 901 310
hoteldaniel.com

MONOCLE COMMENT: If you're feeling adventurous there's a 1950s Silver Creek Clipper van – with a full-size bed and freestanding tub – in the garden.

One of a kind
——
Interiors exude a unique thrift-shop chic

This rooftop bar makes it a little tough to leave...

③
25hours Hotel, Neubau (7th)
Circus-themed fun

25hours Hotel is part of a Hamburg-based hotel group that could teach aspiring chains a thing or two about creating fun accommodation. It may be part of a franchise but everything about this place, from the retail kiosks and the quirky welcome sign to the flea market-sourced furniture, makes it feel like a one-off.

Thanks to its location in the Museumsquartier and rooftop bar with stunning views towards the Ringstrasse and Austrian Parliament Building, 25hours quickly became a hotspot when it opened in 2013. "Everybody feels comfortable here and it's not only tourists who come here – it's also the locals," says Markus Kaplan of BWM Architects which designed the joint.

The 217 rooms are united by a common theme of circus and spectacle: expect bright colours, zany murals on the walls and a photo booth in the lobby. The button-bright service and a roomy downstairs spa in which to unwind are welcome extras. For the peckish there's 1500 Foodmakers restaurant, which serves Italian cuisine: try *caponata siciliana* (Sicilian vegetable stew) and the buratta pizza.
1-3 Lerchenfelder Strasse, 1070
+43 (0)1 521 510
25hours-hotels.com

MONOCLE COMMENT: Plump for one of the XL Rooms: they have bathtubs on the balcony so you can bathe with panoramic views of the 1st district.

Clowning around
———
Each of the unique circus scenes on the hand-painted room walls were created by German illustrator Olaf Hajek. The artist is known for adding a contemporary spin to folkloric images and exploring the hinterland between imagination and reality in western culture.

④
Park Hyatt Vienna,
Innere Stadt (1st)
Bank of luxury

Park Hyatt can't be accused of
conservatism for its first Austrian
property, which it opened in 2014
in the extensively renovated
Golden Quarter. The grand hotel
is located in a 100-year-old former
bank headquarters, a short walk
from the Hofburg Palace.

The 143-room hotel has a
distinctly Viennese flavour –
particularly the excellent food
at the Bank restaurant – but the
overall style is more contemporary
and international than in the city's
older institutions.

The former offices of the bank
director have been turned into
five boardrooms overlooking Am
Hof square and there are plenty
of wood-panelled nooks and
restored spaces in which to enjoy
a coffee. For something stronger
we'd recommend the smart-ish
Pearl Bar.
2 Am Hof, 1010
+43 (0)1 227 401 234
vienna.park.hyatt.com

MONOCLE COMMENT: Pampering
and preening comes in the form of
the Arany Spa and the spectacular
15-metre-long pool, located in the
bank's former vault, is one of the
hotel's best-kept secrets.

⑤
Magdas Hotel, Leopoldstadt (2nd)
On a mission

Vienna has long been a nexus of political, artistic and economic clout but for the most part the city's hotels have been the preserve of the powerful and wealthy. Not so Magdas, which under the control of charitable group Caritas has undertaken a mission to make itself a meeting point for discerning guests and to provide work and shelter for young refugees, many of whom staff the desk and work in the hotel (more than 20 languages are spoken by the 14 nationalities represented here).

The one-time retirement home was built in the 1960s but renovated to its current form with 78 rooms in 2015 by Vienna-based AllesWirdGut architects – the name means, "Everything will be okay".

Inside the lobby – which also functions as a restaurant, bar and living room – the just-so furniture is spare and comforting yet mostly up-cycled and donated. Students from the nearby Academy of Fine Arts also contributed to the design of the space.
12 Laufbergergasse, 1020
+43 (0)1 720 0288
magdas-hotel.at

MONOCLE COMMENT: A rolling artist-in-residence programme ensures that almost every room in the hotel hosts a unique piece of art from the students at the neighbouring Academy of Fine Arts. The winning artists are offered suites by way of reward for their contributions.

I'm off to practise my doggie paddle in the vault

7

Grätzl Hotel, citywide
Lofty ideals

Architects Theresia Kohlmayr, Jonathan Lutter and Christian Knapp opened the first Urbanauts location in Wieden in 2011. After a rebrand in 2015, the Grätzl Hotel group now paves the way for innovative accommodation. The company offers what it dubs street lofts: airy one-room apartments converted from empty shopfronts.

There are 18 spaces and counting, located in central and outer districts. Each is designed in collaboration with BWM Architekten. It's an excellent choice for travellers looking for a pied à terre in some of the city's less trodden 'hoods.
+ 43 (0)1 208 3904
graetzlhotel.com

MONOCLE COMMENT: Each loft is intimately connected to its neighbourhood and special deals for guests are often struck between Grätzl Hotel and nearby markets, shops and restaurants.

6

Hotel Kärntnerhof,
Innere Stadt (1st)
Saucy heritage

Tucked in an alley near St Stephen's Cathedral, this three-star hotel behind a classic 19th-century façade could easily be missed if it weren't for the eye-catching neon sign outside. Once a brothel (military veterans do occasionally wander in, asking "where are the girls?"), the Kärntnerhof has made a name for itself as the smallest of Vienna's grand hotels.

For its 2013 reopening designer Niccolò Grassi and director Nicole Nagel decorated the 44 rooms with custom furniture and a mix of old and new pieces from flea markets and international brands. The hotel lacks a restaurant but its homemade Madame Rosa jam – named for the madam of the old brothel – is a treat, and staff will also happily direct guests to the best bistros in town.
4 Grashofgasse, 1010
+ 43 (0)1 512 1923
karntnerhof.com

MONOCLE COMMENT: Ask to stay in the Dom-Suite for a view of the cathedral; otherwise we'd recommend the Christiane Hörbiger Suite, named after the Austrian TV actress who lives next door and helped design elements of the hotel.

⑧

The Guesthouse, Innere Stadt (1st)
Creature comforts

This hotel is the third collaboration for Austrian entrepreneur Manfred Stallmajer and British interior designer Sir Terence Conran; the duo have also worked together on the respected Das Triest hotel (*see page 24*) and Café Dreschler in the Naschmarkt area.

Located near the Vienna State Opera, this hotel has a classic yet homely feel that offsets its grand surroundings. The building is a one-time hostel with 39 rooms and suites all decorated with Conran's signature flair, and most boast sensational views. Whether it's the standalone bathtubs or handmade soaps from Wolfgang Lederhaas, every detail treads (the right side of) the line between opulence and tastefulness. It's pet friendly too. Pooches are welcome and are even graciously offered a choice of bed size.

Eating at the restaurant and bakery is a must. We recommend the eggs benedict for breakfast and the wiener schnitzel for lunch. You'll need to keep your strength up just to visit all the attractions within walking distance.
10 Führichgasse, 1010
+43 (0)1 512 1320
theguesthouse.at

MONOCLE COMMENT: Suite 802 includes a rooftop terrace with views as far as the city centre, Kahlenberg (Vienna Woods) and Leopoldsberg (a hill some 14km north).

Ⓝ

Hotel Imperial,
Innere Stadt (1st)
Regal riches

Originally home to the Prince of
Württemberg (who was nothing
if not ostentatious) and designed
by architect Arnold Zanetti, this
imposing belle époque build
became a hotel in 1873. Over the
years its 76 rooms and 62 suites
have welcomed the great and the
good, from Austrian composer
Richard Wagner to legendary film
star Charlie Chaplin and the father
of psychoanalysis Sigmund Freud,
who reputedly loved nothing
more than a constitutional along
the Ringstrasse.

As with most hotels of a certain
age, the place has received a few
timely retouches. Coming under
the management of Starwood
Hotels & Resorts in 1998, the hotel
has been faithfully updated to the
most luxurious of standards.

Those not nestling in for the
night can try the homely Café
Imperial, the Opus Restaurant
or the bewilderingly fancy,
fresco-peppered 1873 Hallensalon
Bar – a worthy stop for a sip of
bubbly in the grandest of settings.
16 Kaerntner Ring, 1015
+43 (0)1 501 100
imperialvienna.com

MONOCLE COMMENT: Look up
before you enter the revolving
door outside and you'll see
four statues by sculptor Franz
Melnitzky. Each depicts the
virtues of the ruling Habsburgs
who commissioned him: wisdom,
honour, justice and strength
(from left to right).

Musical history
————
Not only is the hotel
next door to the Viennese
Music Association – home
to the Vienna Philharmonic –
but it also hosts concerts by
talented young musicians,
from jazz groups to opera
singers, in its 1873
Dining Hallensalon Bar.

Ⓝ

Das Triest, Wieden (4th)
Journey's end

This former stagecoach station
connected Vienna to Trieste some
300 years ago but in 1993 it
opened its doors as a 72-room
hotel. The vaulted halls that once
housed stables for horses have
been converted into simple yet
refined suites – some with private
terraces – and charming
conference rooms. Sir Terence
Conran looked after the interiors
(Das Triest was one of his first
ventures into hotel design).

Das Triest has a delightful
Mediterranean-style courtyard
dotted with olive trees. Dining
and drinking is covered by award-
winning chef Josef Neuherz's
restaurant Collio, serving northern
Italian cuisine, and barkeeper Keita
Djibril's Silver Bar. What's more,
it's all within a short stroll of the
Naschmarkt and Vienna's rightly
famed opera house.
12 Wiedner Hauptstrasse, 1040
+43 (0)1 589 180
dastriest.at

MONOCLE COMMENT: Barman
Keita Djibril has created more
than 1,000 cocktails during his 16
or so years at Das Triest. Drop in
for a drink and don't forget to
sample his signature ginger-infused
tipple.

Style council
—
An elegant refit of a stagecoach station

I'm a refined barn owl so this converted five-star stable suits me well

(11)

Altstadt, Neubau (7th)
Theatrical élan

A peculiar plaque showing a
key formed from a loveheart marks
the entrance to the Altstadt hotel
in the artsy Spittelberg district.
Upstairs, the 1902 townhouse
(once a showroom for bathroom
fixtures before becoming a
pension) is now a characterful
45-room hotel.

Each of the rooms is themed
after notable people – including
Italian architect Matteo Thun
and Austrian fashion designer
Lena Hoschek – and is airy,
restful and stocked with
Malin+Goetz amenities. The
hotel sits two blocks to the
west of Vienna's Volkstheater,
the long-established venue dedicated
to staging a range of performances.

The brainchild of Otto E
Wiesenthal, a travelling salesman,
the initial 24-room space opened
in 1991 to fulfil the founder's
dream of running a hotel (and
of having somewhere to stash
his impressive art collection).
Breakfast is a highlight here
and served until 11.30. Expect
Austrian-made Staud's Wien
apricot marmalade, a selection of
Kusmi teas and what might well be
the city's best-cooked breakfast.
41 Kirchengasse, 1070
+ 43 (0)1 522 6666
altstadt.at

MONOCLE COMMENT: Up-and-
coming Spittelberg is home to
shops including S/GHt (*see page 63*)
for womenswear, Die Sellerie
(*see page 50*) for homeware and
restaurant Kussmaul (*see page 28*).

12
Hotel Sacher Wien,
Innere Stadt (1st)
Old-style opulence

The Hotel Sacher Wien has
plied its trade since 1876 and been
under the control of the Gürtler
family since the mid 1930s. Inside
the imposing belle époque shell
there are 149 rooms (some snug,
others palatial) and a top-floor spa.
In the late 1990s, 52 rooms were
added, with extensive renovations
courtesy of French interior
designer Pierre-Yves Rochon.

The hotel's sterling reputation,
however, can be put down to Anna
Sacher, the charismatic owner of
the original hotel who counted
royalty and celebrities of the day
among her clientele in the 38 years
she ran the place. She also started
a convention by which guest's
signatures are embroidered onto
a tablecloth that is on display in
the hotel lobby.

For food we recommend
Rote Bar for a swish sit-down
affair with excellent Viennese
dishes, and the Blaue Bar is apt
for aperitifs. Then there's the
wood-panelled Anna Sacher
restaurant or more informal
street-side Sacher Eck café
for a caffeine fix.
4 Philharmonikerstrasse, 1010
+ 43 (0)1 514 560
sacher.com

MONOCLE COMMENT: In 1969
John Lennon and Yoko Ono
startled the assembled journalists
by conducting an interview from
their room at the Hotel Sacher
Wien. They did so from beneath
a bedsheet. Imagine.

*I'm a high-thread-
count type of pooch...*

Food and drink
—— Capital delights

Viennese cuisine is the only one in the world to be specifically named after a city (rather than a country), which says a lot about its historic roots and significance. It's the capital of strudel, schnitzel, sausages and *sachertorte*. And what would Vienna be without its singular coffeehouse culture, which arrived via the Orient in the 17th century? By the end of the 1800s the city was home to more than 600 cafés; even now you can spend all day in a café corner sipping *melange* (coffee), philosophising and reading the paper.

You'll also find a sausage stand at every corner; we'd recommend sampling the *käsekrainer*, a cheese sausage from Slovenia that was known as *krain* during the days of the Austro-Hungarian empire. Here's our pick of the best food and drink the city has to offer for your next client lunch, cosy coffee break or dinner outing.

Kussmaul, Neubau (7th)
Good-looking in every way

Mario Bernatovic's restaurant, a short walk from the central Maria-Theresien-Platz, is an eye-catcher with its industrial-style interior and Mexican-glass light fixtures. The cuisine is Austrian at heart with a variety of cultural influences inspired by Bernatovic's travels and Croatian roots. It's open for brunch and dinner but good for just a drink too – Kussmaul pours a mean cocktail.
12 Spittelberggasse, 1070
+43 (0)1 5877 6285
kussmaul.at

Farm to table
——
Labstelle sources from nearby producers

2

Labstelle, Innere Stadt (1st)
Classy dining

This Vienna hotspot is tucked away from the commotion of the 1st district in a passage between Lugeck and Wollzeile. Chef Kristijan Bacvanin (*pictured*) is dedicated to creating modern interpretations of Viennese cuisine from the region's best produce. From fish supplied by farmer Franz Hengl to goat's cheese by Helwin Hinke from Vienna Woods, each ingredient is chosen for its quality and provenance.

The design-oriented decor is a delight too; a hanging garden adds greenery to the courtyard while the furniture inside the modish dining space includes classic pieces such as Y-chairs and long dinner tables by Hans J Wegner. *Labstelle* refers to a "feeding place" but this restaurant offers a much more refined experience than its name suggests.
6 Lugeck, 1010
+43 (0)1 236 2122
labstelle.at

I'm getting a taste for this melange malarkey

③

Zum Schwarzen Kameel, Innere Stadt (1st)
Art nouveau flashback

Owner Peter Friese has headed this Viennese institution since 1977 but Kameel (as it's affectionately referred to) has been around for almost four centuries. Kameel remains "one of the most egalitarian places in Vienna", says Friese. "Here a president can sit next to a labourer."

The restaurant had a makeover in 1901 and today is a wonderful example of art nouveau decor with its tiled walls, hanging half-moon lamps and wood panelling. The menu is skewed towards classics such as schnitzel and goulash. In the bar, people sit at the dark-wood counter or stand around chest-high tables eating small sandwiches that were introduced by Friese's late mother. Kameel also has an impressive cellar with more than 800 wines on offer.
5 Bognergasse, 1010
+43 (0)1 5338 12511
kameel.at

④

Spezerei, Leopoldstadt (2nd)
Hole-in-the-wall Italian

Wolfgang Salomon (*pictured*) was inspired to open this homely Italian *osteria* in 2004 with his brother after a stint in Venice. They source their meats, sausages and antipasti directly from Trieste and Venice. The daily menu is simple – usually a choice of two pasta dishes – and diners can watch Salomon cooking on the small stove behind the delicatessen counter. While you wait, we suggest sipping on a glass of wine and leafing through one of the travel books Salomon has authored – look out for the one about Vienna.
2 Karmeliterplatz, 1020
+43 699 1720 0071
spezerei.at

Sausage stands

Despite the sumptuous sit-down meals you'll enjoy in Vienna, some of the city's best food is consumed at the many *würstlstände* (sausage stalls). Stand elbow to elbow with other diners and devour tasty *käsekrainer* (sausages with cheese) or *debreziner* (paprika-spiced sausage).

01 **Bitzinger Wurstlstande, Innere Stadt:** This favourite (*pictured*) is by the entrance to the Albertina museum. You'll find smartly dressed folk sipping Joseph Perrier champagne while enjoying their gourmet sausages at outdoor tables.
bitzinger-wien.at

02 **Hildegard Wurst, citywide:** The idea for selling sausages from an Italian Piaggo Ape van came to Leonie Mayer-Rieckh and Matthias Hofer in 2012. The pair travelled for a month searching for the right ingredients; they ultimately ended up with sausages from Radatz. Keep an eye out for their bright-red truck or visit their deli in Operngasse.
hildegardwurst.at

03 **Kaiserzeit Sausage Stand, Donaustrasse:** Award-winning *blunzn* (blood sausage) and *altwiener suppentopf* (beef noodle broth).
kaiserzeit.wien

⑤
Tian, Innere Stadt (1st)
Vegetarian temple

You'll find this well-dressed vegetarian restaurant across the road from the historical Ronacher Theatre. The completely meat-free dishes are created from ingredients grown in the restaurant's organic garden and have earned it a Michelin star.

The "green" theme is reflected in the decor: the chandeliers are made from birch wood and moss and the walls are adorned with a vibrant collection of plants. Sure, the food is a touch fiddly but it will give you a whole new appreciation for vegetables.
23 Himmelpfortgasse, 1010
+43 (0)1 890 4665
taste-tian.com

6
Vestibül, Innere Stadt (1st)
Royal flavours

In March 2015, chef Jacqueline Pfeiffer joined Christian Domschitz in the kitchen of Vestibül, the opulent dining hall in the Burgtheater's south wing. You'll be dining like royalty (of a kind: this was once the carriage vestibule of the emperor's court theatre), surrounded by marble columns, dramatic archways with gothic details and flickering candlelight. Pairing Pfeiffer's offbeat cooking with Domschitz's Austro-French background has resulted in a menu that features traditional Austrian dishes with a contemporary twist.

The menu changes according to the seasons but there is one house speciality that remains constant: the lobster and cabbage dressed in paprika cream sauce. Domschitz has been cooking the dish for more than 20 years.
Universitätsring 2, 1010
+43 (0)1 532 4999
vestibuel.at

Too. Many.
Sausages. I
just need a
moment...

7
Petz im Gusshaus, Wieden (4th)
Cooking up a storm

Chef Christian Petz is an expert in creative cookery. There's *vitello dorschato* (veal with cod-liver sauce), beef tatare and for the adventurous, calf's-heart steak in apple-balsam sauce with *spätzle* (soft egg noodles). Before opening his own restaurant, Petz cooked at Michelin-starred establishment the Palais Coburg Residenz. In 2009 he started making chocolate too. His brand is called Xocolat and you can savour some of his homemade pralines that go exceptionally well with a chilled glass of riesling.
23 Gusshausstrasse, 1040
+43 (0)1 504 4750
gusshaus.at

Mix it up
—
Diners can have multiple dishes in the same pot

8
Mama Liu & Sons, Mariahilf (6th)
Hot-pot hotspot

Mama Liu Mine and her sons Liu Yong and Liu Feng create mouthwatering home-cooked goodies at this restaurant that's just a short walk from the Naschmarkt. Our pick of the dinner menu is the hot pot that you cook yourself on the table: select a soup base, throw in a selection of vegetables, seafood or meat and let it all sizzle away. You can even choose from a variety of soup bases thanks to the multi-cavity pots. Keep in mind that the hot pots are only available on the dinner menu.

Vienna-based design firm Tzou Lubroth Architekten created the serene dining space, setting the scene with exposed brick walls featuring traditional Chinese artworks and dim lighting. It does get busy so grab a perch at the bar and pop the top off a Lucky Beer if you have to wait for a table.
29 Gumpendorfer Strasse 1060
+43 (0)1 586 3673
mamaliuandsons.at

Top markets

01 Naschmarkt, Mariahilf:
The spice, dried fruit and
nut stands, bartering stall
vendors and wafts of fresh
falafel may well make you
think that you're in the
middle of a Middle Eastern
market if it weren't for the
palatial mansions lining the
Wienzeile and the neatly
stocked Viennese produce.
Dating from the 1600s, this
spot is a popular meeting
place for young and old,
especially on Saturday when
it turns into a flea market.
Naschmarkt, 1060

02 Karmelitermarkt,
Leopoldsgasse: This
is where residents and
restaurateurs purchase
fresh fruit and vegetables,
as well as delicatessen
from the likes of Kaas am
Markt and Zimmer 37.
The colourful market stalls
highlight the multicultural
mix of the neighbourhood:
cheese and bread stands
sit next to kosher butchers
and halal meat stalls.
Karmelitermarkt, 1020

Motto am Fluss, Innere Stadt (1st)
Come on in

This welcoming restaurant sits within the Wien-City ferry terminal and boasts lovely views over the Donaukanal. There are two venues sharing the space: a classy yet welcoming 1950s-style restaurant and a breezy café that boasts a spectacular deck area.

Come nightfall the cocktail bar in the restaurant thrums, often set to lively accompaniment from a resident DJ (the owners are also behind a well-regarded nightclub, called Motto, located in Vienna's Margareten in the southwest of the city).
2 Schwedenpl, 1010
+43 (0)1 252 5510
motto.at

The Brickmakers Pub and Kitchen, Neubau (7th)
Beer frontier

Irish-born Brian Patton relocated to Vienna in 1997 to open his bar Charlie P's. Eighteen years later he launched The Brickmakers, inspired by the US craft beer revolution, and his popular pop-up barbecue restaurant Big Smoke. Leave Vienna at the door and say hello to the Wild West as you take a seat in the Western-style tavern bar with a cold pint of the house-brewed ale and some slow-cooked smoky beef brisket.

With 30 craft beers on tap and a further 150 in bottles – many of them Austrian – there's no lack of choice. "We specialise in ales and ciders and I actually make my own beer," says Patton. Best of all, Michelin-starred chef Peter Zinter has perfected the delicate art of the smoked barbecue, which makes this venue stand out.
42 Zieglergasse, 1070
+43 (0)1 997 4414
brickmakers.at

Skopik + Lohn, Leopoldstadt (2nd)
Wiener wonders

"If you were to imagine what a restaurant in New York would look like if it were opened by a Viennese immigrant, that is what I aimed for," says chef Horst Scheuer. Since he and his wife Connie launched Skopik + Lohn in 2006, they've raked in accolades for their hearty Austrian menu that also bears a strong French bent (you'll find beef tartare and coq au vin alongside blood sausage). The dining room's dramatic "scribble" theme is courtesy of artist Otto Zitko. Our pick is the excellent wiener schnitzel and potato salad.
17 Leopoldsgasse, 1020
+43 (0)1 219 8977
skopikundlohn.at

⑫

Pizza Mari, Leopoldstadt (2nd)
Taste of Naples

It was a prolonged stay in Naples,
where she had her first taste of real
pizza, that inspired Maria Fuchs
to open Pizza Mari upon her
return to Vienna in 2008. The
centrepiece of this southern
Italian restaurant is the authentic
wood-fired oven. Fuchs prides
herself on serving Neapolitan-style
fare: "The most important things are
high-quality ingredients, the
knowledge of the *pizzaiolo* [pizza
chef] and the temperature of the
oven," she says.

The pizza here steals the show
and the restaurant is always
bustling but the wait is never long
as speedy waiters wearing aprons
designed by Fuchs's mother dash
from table to table. Grab a spot
outside if the weather is fine. Just
opposite the pizzeria you'll find
Fuchs's Super Mari, a sleek
Italian café-cum-shop.
23A Leopoldsgasse, 1020
+ 43 676 687 4994
pizzamari.at

Slice of Italy
—
The pizza
is cooked in
the Naples
tradition

⑬
Neni, Mariahilf (6th)
Hearty Israeli dishes

Chef Haya Molcho runs five restaurants around the world with the help of her four sons Nuriel, Elior, Nadiv and Ilan ("Neni" is an acronym of their initials). This outpost in the Naschmarkt opened in 2010. "When it came to the location I knew it had to be at a market," says Molcho. "Talking to farmers and merchants is where I draw my inspiration."

The Israeli cuisine includes staples such as kebabs and mezze plates. We recommend starting your day with a hearty breakfast of fresh labneh, eggs, pita and salad.
510 Naschmarkt, 1060
+43 (0)1 585 2020
neni.at

I always rest my wings at Neni when visiting the Naschmarkt

Must-try
Sarma at Zur Herknerin, Wieden
These cabbage rolls stuffed with mincemeat made their way to Europe during the Middle Ages where they've since become a classic, particularly in Vienna. The best place to enjoy them is at Stefanie Herkner's Zur Herknerin. "I wanted to create a place where Austrian and Viennese food tastes like it tasted when we were kids," she says. Her menu changes daily but Sarma is her number-one dish.
zurherknerin.at

Global gourmet
Neni is as international as the offerings around the Naschmarkt; the family has restaurants in Berlin, Zürich, Hamburg and Tel Aviv. In case the market is too far for you, drop by your nearest Spar supermarket where you'll find Neni's falafel and hummus on the shelves.

⑭
Meierei, Landstrasse (3rd)
Classy quick bites

Meierei is the more casual sister of chef Heinz Reitbauer's world-famous Steirereck restaurant. The Viennese say it's the home of the city's best *kaiserschmarrn* (shredded pancake) and you'll also find traditional Austrian soups, pastries and stews, and a selection of more than 120 cheeses from around the world. We recommend the refined breakfast of poached duck egg with Perigord truffle and watercress. Follow it up with a wander in the Stadtpark; the restaurant is located in the old milk-drinking hall in the centre of the grounds.
2A Am Heumarkt, 1030
+43 (01) 713 3168
steirereck.at/meierei/

Wash it down
—
Pfarrwirt has its own working vineyard

Must-try
Georgian breakfast at Café Ansari, Leopoldstadt
The family-run Café Ansari serves a fusion of Middle Eastern and co-owner Nina Ansari's native-Georgian cuisines. The restaurant is a modern take on the traditional Viennese coffeehouse. Start your day with the papers and a Georgian breakfast: a mouthwatering dough dumpling filled with creamy mozzarella, topped with a fried egg and accompanied by a cherry-tomato salad drizzled with red basil dressing.
cafeansari.at

⑮
Pfarrwirt, Döbling (19th)
History repeating

Vienna's oldest restaurant, the Pfarrwirt, is housed in a building that dates back to the 12th century and lies in the shadow of historic Saint Jakob's Church. Meals are served in three gothic and Baroque-style rooms; the beautiful wooden porch was added in 1872 to reflect Vienna's popular coffee culture. Take a seat in "Beethoven's favourite spot" and let the kitchen spoil you with classics such as prime boiled beef and wiener schnitzel. It may be a 20-minute drive from the centre of town but this feast is well worth the trip.
5 Pfarrplatz, 1190
+43 (0)1 370 7373
pfarrwirt.com

I'm quite partial to a spritzer or two at brunch

Lip service
—
First settled in 1675, the cultural and culinary neighbourhood surrounding Kussmaul is worth exploring. Once likened to Pigalle in Paris, its red-light district days are long gone (although "Kussmaul" references its salacious past: it means "kiss-mouth").

Coffee
Café culture

①
Balthasar, Leopoldstadt (2nd)
Raising the bar

Halfway down Praterstrasse and a short walk from the giant Ferris wheel you'll smell Balthasar's freshly brewed coffee. Otto Bayer, whose family has been in the catering business for more than a century, opened this coffeeshop in reaction to those Viennese establishments that serve coffee without giving the process a second thought. Not so at Balthasar, where the art of good coffee is the be-all and end-all.

The coffee counter and the La Marzocco Strada machine take centre stage in the café, which has been serving flat whites and cold brews to an enthusiastic clientele since 2014. Balthasar's own house blends, such as the signature Colombia single origin Balthasar No32, are superb. Add a slice of freshly baked cake from Felzl and your afternoon is complete.
38 Praterstrasse, 1020
+43 664 381 6855
balthasar.at

②
Café Landtmann, Innere Stadt (1st)
Coffee craft

One of the most prominent and opulent coffeehouses in Vienna is Landtmann, on the ground floor of the Palais Lieben-Auspitz by the Burgtheater. It's a place where a casual coffee break entails a perfectly foamed *melange* served in monogrammed cups with gold handles, and an abundance of finely crafted desserts.

The café was founded by Franz Landtmann in 1873 and soon became a favourite haunt of the likes of Gustav Mahler and Sigmund Freud, as well as glamorous visiting celebrities such as Marlene Dietrich. The type of clientele hasn't changed much and it is pretty common to find yourself sitting side by side with the most prominent artists, politicians and businessmen in Vienna. From Sunday to Tuesday there is live piano music from 20.00 to 23.00.
4 Universitätsring, 1010
+43 (0)1 2410 0100
landtmann.at

Café Prückel, Innere Stadt (1st)
Old-school glamour

Café Prückel is a hotspot for both the well heeled and bohemian types who fill its weathered banquettes from morning until night. Originally designed in the colourful, dreamy style of Austrian artist Hans Makart when it opened in 1904, its interior was later updated by architect Oswald Haerdtl, resulting in the 1950s-inspired decor that is so beloved today.

Its large windows are perfect for people-watching over breakfast – we recommend the traditional *wiener frühstück* (Viennese breakfast) and the apple strudel – and you can get stuck into a wide selection of newspapers. For those who smoke, there is a designated area. In the evenings, reasonably priced dishes such as goulash and potato salad are sure winners, while frequent piano concerts keep guests entertained.
24 Stubenring, 1010
+43 (0)1 512 6115
prueckel.at

Now that's what I call a schnitzel!

Café society

Regulars include author Michael Köhlmeier

④
Café Sperl, Wieden (4th)
Brewed to perfection

With its elegant engraved panelling, parquet floors, wooden chairs and low-hanging lamps, Café Sperl, which was established in 1880, is the definition of a traditional coffeehouse. The beauty of Viennese cafés is that they invite you to linger – you won't be rushed to give up your table – and there is no better place to while away the hours. The seats are comfortable, the coffee is strong and the atmosphere extremely relaxed.

Catch up on the news (there are a host of newspapers and weeklies to select from, such as *Der Standard* and *The Economist*) while you wait for your *melange* and a slice of the signature *sperltorte*, an almond-and-chocolate-cream concoction. If you're not in a hurry you can play a round of billiards or just watch the world go by.
11 Gumpendorfer Strasse, 1060
+43 (0)1 586 4158
cafesperl.at

Talk of the town
—
Try the nougat and chocolate torte

⑤
Demel, Innere Stadt (1st)
Royal delights

Walk down the pedestrianised
Kohlmarkt and the aroma of fresh
pastry and other sweet treats will
alert you to Demel's location.
Dating back to 1786, the imperial
confectioner's name is synonymous
with beautifully packaged cakes and
chocolate. Order a *melange* and
apfelstrudel (apple strudel) and watch
your order being made by an army
of pâtissiers. The neo-Baroque shop
is stacked high with the famous
chocolates called *langues de chat*
(cats' tongues), always an essential
Viennese addition to both your
suitcase and your stomach.
14 Kohlmarkt, 1010
+ 43 (0)1 5351 7170
demel.at

6

Café Sacher, Innere Stadt (1st)
Opulent outing

Café Sacher is located in the five-star Hotel Sacher Wien across from the historical Vienna State Opera. Head here for a generous portion of the decadent *sachertorte*, which includes chocolate and a thin but vital layer of apricot jam (the original recipe remains a secret). This is the famous dessert's natural home – both hotel and café were founded in 1876 by Eduard Sacher, son of the creator of the *sachertorte*. With plush burgundy sofas and twinkling chandeliers, the café is defined by its *gemütlichkeit* (cosiness), making it an ideal spot to soak up a little Viennese charm.
4 Philharmoniker Strasse, 1010
+43 (0)1 514 560
sacher.com

Piece of cake

The *sachertorte* came to fame through a lucky accident. In 1832 Prince Metternich threw a dinner party, but when his chef fell ill his 16-year-old apprentice Franz Sacher had to step in. That evening *sachertorte* celebrated its debut and has been served around the world ever since.

7
CaffèCouture, Innere Stadt (1st)
Quest for coffee

Old-school cafés serving
questionable coffee have been
challenged in recent years by
more serious third-wave coffee
offerings. Located on Ferstel
Passage, a Baroque arcade within a
one-time bank and stock exchange,
is CaffèCouture. Founded by
barista Georg Branny, the simple
space serves great flat whites
and top-notch espressos using
equipment from Hario, Chemex
and Aeropress. Branny really
knows his stuff: he's a multiple
Austrian Barista Champion and
roasts his own coffee.
2 Freyung, 1010
+43 676 332 2076
caffecouture.com

Gelaterias
Cool sensations

①
Eis-Greissler, Innere Stadt (1st)
Scoop of the day

Georg and Andrea Blochberger's
45 cows are their "most important
members of staff". Originally selling
milk and yoghurt from their dairy
farm to schools and restaurants,
they started experimenting with ice
cream and opened their first parlour
in 2011. They create more than 100
flavours such as poppy seed,
pumpkin seed and elderflower, as
well as vegan ice cream.
    The original shop on
Rotenturmstrasse serves scoops
from March through to December,
while an outlet on Mariahilferstrasse
opens from March until the end
of September.
14 Rotenturmstrasse, 1010
eis-greissler.at

②
Ice Dream Factory, Neubau (7th)
Imaginative scoops

For a taste of the US, step inside Carsten Eickhoff's Ice Dream Factory. "I like 'American-style' ice cream with lots of chunks and swirls in it," says Eickhoff, who opened the parlour in 2013 and makes everything on the premises from scratch, including the cones, to ensure the highest quality.

The simple wooden counter gives the place a rustic, laidback air and the smell of fresh homemade waffles is mouth-watering. Indulge your sweet tooth with a scoop ot two of the uniquely named Pink Panther, Killing Me Softly or Mother's Nightmare – chocolate ice cream with brownie chunks and homemade peanut butter – and don't forget the sprinkles. On a sunny day, grab a seat outside, rest your feet and get ready for a sugary rush to the head.
68 Burggasse, 1070
+43 699 1826 4697
icedreamfactory.com

Lunch
Midday bites

❶
Trzesniewski, Innere Stadt (1st)
Spreads and breads

Specialising in open-top sandwiches (*brötchen*), the 100-year-old Trzesniewski is an institution loved by city residents and tourists alike. Manned by a small army of yellow-and-white pinafored matrons, its long glass counters groan under the weight of picture-perfect rectangular sandwiches. Choose from 22 different types of mayonnaise-based spreads – including egg, mushroom, herring, liver, crab and tomato – then order a miniature stein of Pfiff beer. Don't expect a table: seating is limited and most people stand at the counter.
1 Dorotheergasse, 1010
+43 (0)1 512 3291
trzesniewski.at

Ice age
The first gelaterias arrived in Vienna from Italy during the 19th century. Since then more than 110 ice cream parlours have popped up across the capital, crowning Vienna as the city with the highest concentration of ice cream shops in all of Europe.

Brötchen washed down with a stein or two: the perfect lunch

2
Tanzen Anders, Margareten (5th)
Recipe for success

Chef David Gemeinböck
(*pictured, above*) named this
minimalist brunch spot after
a song by Vienna's late pop-and-
rock legend Falco, who lived in
the area. The excellent, low-key
menu and relaxed charm make
this an inviting spot to relax in
after a hard day's sightseeing.
Choose from coffee that's roasted
on-site, homemade soups, burgers,
salads and pastries.
  "One of our favourite dishes
is The Elvis: toast with roasted
banana, peanut butter and crispy
bacon," says Gemeinböck.
29 Ziegelofengasse, 1050
+43 (0)1 974 4774
tanzenanders.at

Room to grow
——
The café
caters for
vegans
too

③
Joseph Brot vom Pheinsten, Landstrasse (3rd)
Nice buns

Josef Weghaupt seems to have discovered the recipe for perfect bread. An adherent of traditional craftsmanship, he only uses 100 per cent organic demeter grain. His fluffy croissants and delicately flavoured apple torte with a hint of cinnamon hit the spot every time. You can also pick up jams and spreads, as well as an organic coffee, to go with your pastries.

In addition to a bakery in Innere Stadt and a patisserie in Döbling, Weghaupt runs this buzzing organic bistro-cum-bakery in the 3rd district that serves breakfast, lunch and dinner. If you're feeling in need of a pick-me-up after a night on the tiles, opt for the Queen Elizabeth Hangover breakfast that includes traditionally made *britwurst aus österreich*, scrambled eggs, potatoes and grilled tomatoes.
4 Landstrasser Hauptstrasse, 1030
+43 (0)1 710 2881
joseph.co.at

④
Marco Simonis-Bastei 10, Innere Stadt (1st)
Best of both worlds

Combining two of the greatest joys of life, eating and shopping, Marco Simonis-Bastei 10 opened its doors in 2014. Founder Marco Simonis has an extensive background in the catering industry and found that a certain kind of experience, one that can be found in cities such as London, New York, Paris and Tokyo, was missing in Vienna. Bastei 10 was his solution.

The concept shop mixes food and design to appease urbanite appetites, providing a selection of design products from selected labels in Scandinavia, France, Italy and the UK. The food is made using seasonal organic ingredients ranging from appetising pastas and crispy croissants to fragrant coffee and daily lunch treats.
10 Dominikanerbastei, 1010
+43 (0)1 512 2010
marcosimonis.com

⑤
Gasthaus Pöschl, Innere Stadt (1st)
Home from home

Food journalist, cook and wife of founder Hanno Pöschl, Andrea Karrer-Pöschl is the captain of this wholesome and quintessentially Viennese ship. It has simple wood tables, whitewashed walls, a menu that is consistently excellent and an extremely loyal clientele, so we recommend making a reservation in advance. Traditional and delicious home cooking is a promise kept by the kitchen. The menu changes daily but expect dishes such as goulash and calves' liver. Wash it down with beer or wine produced in the vicinity of Vienna.
17 Weihburggasse, 1010
+43 (0)1 513 5288

Hmmm, can I fit any more tortes into my bag?

① If Dogs Run Free, Mariahilf (6th)
Cocktail culture

"If dogs run free, then why not we?" sang Bob Dylan in the 1970s. Architects Gregorio Lubroth and Chieh-shu Tzou picked up his lead and in 2012 opened a bar named after this bluesy tune, conveniently located next door to their practice. The architects exerted themselves in creating a ceiling that resembles a snowy mountainscape, inspired by illustrations in Chinese art.

It can be a tad difficult to find a small, friendly cocktail bar in Vienna, so this hole-in-the-wall offering is all the more special. The cocktail list is inventive and unusual, but it's hard to look past a superb Old Fashioneds.
10 Gumpendorfer Strasse, 1060
+ 43 (0)1 913 2132
ifdogsrunfree.com

② Die Rundbar, Neubau (7th)
Vintage flair

The 7th district is Vienna's artsy quarter, with plenty of small galleries and boutiques, and Die Rundbar has been a great addition. From the colourful stained glass behind the mahogany bar to the cubist chandelier, fabric wallpaper and vintage armchairs, this bar references the 1950s; the results are warm and charming rather than kitschy. A café during the day, it turns into a cocktail bar in the evening that is always buzzing with conversation and music.

Behind the bar is Roland Wagner, who mixes well-crafted Moscow Mules, Gimlets and his cava ginger creations. The kitchen is run by Italian chef Andrea Cipriano, who creates delicacies such as octopus gazpacho and scallops. Dishes are on the small side so order a few to share; you won't regret it.
1 Lindengasse, 1070
+ 43 (0)1 522 4447
dierundbar.com

③ Unger und Klein, Innere Stadt (1st)
Wine connoisseurs

Unger und Klein, a bar-cum-shop, is a meeting place for wine lovers who are looking for something new in Vienna's textile quarter. With a global selection of the best wines along with Austria's top bottles, husband-and-wife owners Helmuth Unger (*pictured*) and Michi Klein have created a pleasant little bar where a selection of 50 wines is served by the glass, along with nibbles such as nuts and salami. Competition for good wine may be stiff in Vienna but Unger and Klein are still regarded as the experts on the city's wine scene.
2 Gölsdorfgasse, 1010
+ 43 (0)1 532 1323
ungerundklein.at

Top heurigen

Viennese *heurigen* (taverns), where wine from the latest harvest is served, are famous around the world. Here are three of our favourites.

01 Sirbu, Döbling: The origins of this *heuriger* can be traced back to 1688. It's one of the oldest taverns in Nussdorf and offers breathtaking views across Vienna.
sirbu.at

02 Mayer am Pfarrplatz, Döbling: This vineyard in Heiligenstadt, near the banks of the Danube, has a long history and bottles award-winning riesling.
pfarrplatz.at

03 Christ Vineyards, Floridsdorf: The combination of contemporary architecture, four centuries of family tradition and wooden-barrel-aged wine makes this *heuriger* on the northern banks of the Danube an institution.
weingut-christ.at

④
Volksgarten Pavillon,
Innere Stadt (1st)
Music to our ears

This 1950s-style pavilion with views of Heldenplatz is a perfect place to stop off for a coffee. You might be in the city centre but you will feel as though you are at a garden party, surrounded by soaring trees and colourful flowers. Come here in the evening for drinks and to hear top DJs; the highlight is the legendary Tuesday-night techno party. During the summer months the pavilion also hosts barbecues; head chef Matthias Zykan cooks up a feast on an oversized grill.
Volksgarten, 1010
+43 (0)1 532 0907
volksgarten-pavillon.at

⑤
Zum Gschupften Ferdl,
Mariahilf (6th)
Game on

Entrepreneurs Nick Pöschl, Stephan Csiszar and the founders of denim brand Gebrüder Stitch opened this organic rendition of a traditional *heuriger* in 2014. To give it an edge, the decor was conceived to resemble an old-school video game: you'll find pixel-inspired neon signs and geometric furnishings. Sit back with a glass of *grüner veltliner*, tuck into popular starter *brettljausen* – a smorgasbord of cheese and sausage delicacies – and tap along to the jukebox.
20 Windmühlgasse, 1060
+43 (0)1 966 3066
zumgschupftnferdl.com

Let's get this heuriger rocking!

Retail
—— Masterful purchases

Vienna is not associated with shopping to the extent of London, Paris and New York yet the world of retail could learn a lot from the Austrian capital. Here centuries-old family-run shops such as shoemaker Rudolf Scheer & Söhne and tailor Knize set the mark for craftsmanship. Whether it's a hat from master milliner Mühlbauer or a set of porcelain plates from Feinedinge, the city offers a disproportionate number of places to buy specialist goods made using traditional techniques, time-honed designs and quality ingredients. But that's not to say the scene is stuck in the past; a bevy of independent boutiques, including concept store Song and fashion-forward Park, are bringing a breath of fresh air to the retail selection.

The density of shops is at its greatest in the 1st district but promising purveyors are peppered across the city. And no visit would be complete without experiencing the capital's historical and vibrant food markets.

So read on for our favourite shopping spots.

Concept
Out-of-the-box shops

①
Park, Neubau (7th)
Work of art

This gallery-inspired space in the 7th district's Mondscheingasse presents its collection of clothing and accessories like artworks. Co-founders Helmut Ruthner and Markus Strasser – formerly of Jil Sander – showcase designer and streetwear, including pieces by Maison Martin Margiela, Ann Demeulemeester, John Smedley and Austrian-born Carolin Lerch's label Pelican Avenue.

You'll also find original Eames chairs, stacks of art-and-design books, jewellery by Raf Simons and shoes by Roberto Del Carlo.
20 Mondscheingasse, 1070
+ 43 (0)1 526 4414
park.co.at

I'd say this is an open-and-shut case, officer

②

Supersense, Leopoldstadt (2nd)
Old-school creative space

Nina Ugrinovich, Andreas Hoeller
and Florian Kaps (*all pictured,*
Kaps on right) founded Supersense
in 2008 as a workroom and
playground for creative types.
"It's an analogue palace," says
Kaps. In this shop-cum-café,
housed in a 19th-century Venetian-
style palazzo, a range of analogue
tools come together. You can
print a poster or record your own
vinyl track in the Flabbergasting
Record Elevator before taking
a break for a *handsemmel mit*
beinschinken (ham roll). Let
your imagination run wild.
70 Praterstrasse, 1020
+43 (0)1 969 0832
supersense.com

Just our type
———
Those who appreciate a good
typeface can have custom
posters and postcards printed
using an antique Korrex
letterpress, while Wild Evel offers
a handwriting and drawing
service by appointment for
anything requiring a personal
touch – from love letters
to invites.

Grand designs
———
Supersense
is in a 19th-
century
palazzo

4

Vienna to Go, Mariahilf (6th)
Sophisticated mementoes

Vienna to Go is a souvenir shop with a difference: for a start, it's located in Otto Wagner's magnificent art nouveau Majolikahaus building opposite the Naschmarkt. "I am tired of the usual Vienna souvenirs," says owner Karen Gröbner, a German graphic designer. "They are kitsch, poor quality and expensive." Instead Gröbner sells items made by her students, including purses and clutches by Johannes Lerch, alongside books by Austrian publisher Metroverlag. Homeware and Gröbner's own quirky postcards are also on offer.
Unit 40, 12 Linke Wienzeile, 1060
+ 43 699 1944 0859
vienna-to-go.at

3

Kaufhaus Wall, Neubau (7th)
Cut above

Kaufhaus Wall, formerly known as Be a Good Girl, combines a retail space with a hairdressing salon, making it a one-stop shop if you're after an image overhaul. In the clothing section you'll find independent labels such as Copenhagen-based brands First Aid to the Injured and The Last Conspiracy alongside established names from Germany, Scandinavia and Switzerland. Owner Andreas Wall is passionate about supporting Viennese brands such as Das Goldene Wiener Herz and Lederhaas; there's also a fine selection of art and design books and grooming products.
5a Westbahnstrasse, 1070
+ 43 (0)1 524 4728
kaufhauswall.com

1

Die Sellerie, Nebau (7th)
Stationery of note

This snug shop in the Museumsquartier was launched in 2010 by graphic designers Patrick Bauer (*pictured*), Ulrike Dorner and Georg Leditzky to create and sell a line of stationery, fine-art prints, home accessories and gifts. "We wanted to position ourselves as a Viennese alternative to the big players of home decor and create a cosy space," says Leditzky. Besides its own-brand stationery collection, the shop's stock ranges from Austrian Aeijst gin to candle-holders by Denmark's Nicholas Oldroyd Design.
Unit 21, 1 Burggasse, 1070
+ 43 699 1210 9304
diesellerie.com

Set in place
—
Feinedinge makes ceramics for the table

(3) Wiener Silber Manufactur, Innere Stadt (1st)
Sharp design

This table-silverware maker is a cut above the rest. Its workshop taps into 130 years of tradition in the craft, using models and tools that date back to 1882, when the company was founded. After a relaunch in 2009 the brand has shone anew, using a silver alloy of 940/000 that retains a classic look while being hardy enough for the dishwasher. Its shop houses some 11,000 drawings in its archive, as well as contemporary designs by the likes of Zaha Hadid and Erwin Wurm.
*1-3 Schwarzenbergstrasse, 1010
+43 (0)1 513 4567
wienersilbermannfactur.com*

Perhaps it's a silver napkin ring from Wiener Silber?

(2) Feinedinge, Wieden (4th)
Pretty porcelain pieces

Sandra Haischberger's ceramics studio of "fine things" presides on Margaretenstrasse, minutes from the Naschmarkt. Its display windows are lit by the shop's signature spherical Moonstruck lamps and everywhere you turn cups, plates and teapots adorn shelves and tables.

The best bit is the open studio that's visible from the shop floor, where Haischberger and her five-strong team handcraft porcelain bowls and candle-holders in a plethora of colours, constantly feeding the kiln with a new load. Everything they produce has its imperfections but that is where the beauty lies. "Our pieces are not meant to be packed away in a glass cabinet, they're meant to be used," says Haischberger. "Our craftsmanship is visible so they're all one-of-a-kind."
*35 Margaretenstrasse, 1040
+43 (0)1 954 0918
feinedinge.at*

④

J & L Lobmeyr, Innere Stadt (1st)
Dazzling craftsmanship

As much a museum of the art
of glass-making as a seller of fine
crystal, J & L Lobmeyr is a lavish
and ornate treasure trove in which
you'll find chandeliers, mirrors
and glassware. It has occupied its
position at the centre of Vienna's
main shopping thoroughfare,
Kärntner Strasse, for nearly 200
years, and its heritage is reflected
in its stock. The business is run by
a trio of brothers who are the sixth-
generation of their family to do so.

The shop is peppered with
Hungarian Herend porcelain and
Biedermeier pieces, while drinking
sets by Adolf Loos sit alongside more
modern pieces by designers such as
Claesson Koivisto Rune and Polka.
J & L Lobmeyr has a client list that
has included the Austrian royal family.
Many of the handmade items on offer
are created by craftsmen using
ancient, increasingly rare techniques.
26 Kärntner Strasse, 1010
+ 43 (0)1 512 0508
lobmeyr.at

I'm not sure a
horse-drawn
carriage
is the best
way to avoid
breakages…

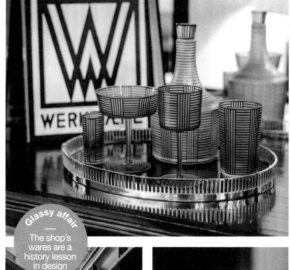

Glassy affair
———
The shop's
wares are a
history lesson
in design

⑦
Zur Schwäbischen Jungfrau, Innere Stadt (1st)
Heritage homeware seller

This 300-year-old business boasts an illustrious clientele, including Archduchess Maria Theresa, Empress Sissi and most recently the king of Malaysia. Hanni Vanicek (*pictured*), who took over the business in 1959 after starting as an apprentice, has handed the reins to her nephew Theodor but you'll still find her bustling around the three cosy floors. Handcrafted wares on offer include napkins, bedsheets, cushions, cashmere blankets and lace tablecloths.
26 Graben, 1010
+43 (0)1 535 5356
schwaebische-jungfrau.at

⑥
Wittmann, Innere Stadt (1st)
Part of the furniture

This family-run furniture company, now in its fourth generation under Ulrike Wittmann and her husband Heinz Hofter-Wittmann, branched out from saddlery into upholstered furnishings in the early 1960s. Today, the company is represented in more than 40 countries.

Headquartered in the Krems-Land District northwest of Vienna, it has particular expertise in making bespoke sofas, chairs, beds and tables. The firm works with designers and artists from home and abroad, such as Italy's Matteo Thun, co-founder of the Memphis Group design movement, and Vienna-based Marco Dessi. Fine materials and exacting handiwork mean Wittmann's pieces, such as celebrated Austrian designer Josef Hoffmann's geometric Kubus armchair, are built to last.
10 Friedrichstrasse, 1010
+43 (0)1 585 7725
wittmann.at

⑤
Lichterloh, Mariahilf (6th)
Pieces of history

This furniture emporium combines restored modernist pieces with contemporary pieces made by owners and founders Dagmar Moser, Philipp-Markus Pernhaupt and Christof Stein. "Our focus is 20th-century furniture from the 1920s to 1970s," says Moser (*pictured*).

The chairs, cabinets, tables and lamps are picked up at European vintage markets from Italy to France and restored in the team's workshop in Vienna. Moser is particularly fond of pieces such as the embellished iron hallstands and Roland Rainer-designed Stadthallensessel stacking chairs that formerly graced Vienna's concert hall. "Every piece tells a story and documents history," she says. You can pop around the corner to the famous Café Sperl (*see page 39*) when you're done perusing.
15-17 Gumpendorfer Strasse, 1060
+43 (0)1 586 0520
lichterloh.com

(8)

Vintagerie, Mariahilf (6th)
Quirky design pieces

A former clothing factory now hosts this collection of rare furniture from the 1930s to 1980s. Expect to find chandeliers by Kalmar and Lobmeyr, Walter Bosse brass lamps and the odd classic Ottakringer Leiterstuhl chair. "Design has great history here in Vienna and we like to focus on Austrian pieces," says Peter Lindenberg, who met co-founder Alexander Bechstein while shopping for curiosities at a flea market. The pair quickly became friends over regular Friday-night drinks of sparkling rosé. To uphold this tradition, every visitor to the vintage-design shop is greeted with a glass of bubbly.
4 Nelkengasse, 1060
+43 (0)1 581 2850
vintagerie.at

(9)

Jarosinski & Vaugoin, Neubau (7th)
Sterling history

The heritage of this silverware firm is palpable as soon as you step inside its *fin de siècle* premises. "We have a rich background and thousands of sketches and pictures that we draw inspiration from," says Jean-Paul Vaugoin (*pictured*), who is the sixth generation of the family to preside over the company since it was founded in 1847. Visitors can marvel at Vaugoin's own elaborate tableware and flatware and Thomas Feichtner's 2013-designed *sahera* (salt cellar) based on Benvenuto Cellini's masterpiece.
24 Zieglergasse, 1070
+43 (0)1 523 3388
vaugoin.com

Wien Products
—
Vienna is a city rich with design talent, long prized for generating works of quality, flair and finesse. Wien Products brings together and supports a roster of innovative and traditional creations from silverware and furniture to glassware and jewellery, all made in the capital.
wienproducts.at

Specialist retail
Niche goods

①
Rudolf Scheer & Söhne, Innere Stadt (1st)
Europe's oldest shoemaker

During imperial times, members of the Habsburg monarchy beat a path to this bespoke shoemaker. It is now run by Markus Scheer, the seventh generation of his family to have headed the firm since it was founded in 1816.

In the stately shop's first-floor atelier, 15 cobblers make sure that bespoke Scheer footwear is an investment that will last a lifetime (commissions begin at €5,000). The designs range from smart dress shoes (Oxfords and Derbies) to wingtips and boots.

Pop into the firm's two new adjoining showrooms that offer leather accessories, shoe-cleaning kits and homeware – including a reproduction of the original light that shoemakers used two centuries ago to cobble well into the early hours of the morning.
4 Bräunerstrasse, 1010
+43 (0)1 533 8084
scheer.at

R Horn's Wien, Innere Stadt (1st)
Personalised leathergoods

In the shadow of St Stephen's Cathedral, R Horn's stocks some of Vienna's most covetable accessories, including bags, wallets, pouches, briefcases and holdalls made using the finest nubuck, calf leather or scotch grain (a rough, tough cowhide) sourced from Italian tanneries.

The designs are influenced by Otto Wagner, Adolf Loos and the Wiener Werkstätte arts-and-crafts movement. R Horn's bags can be personalised to suit any customer. As a finishing touch, products are lined with moiré silk or suede.
3 Stephansplatz, 1010
+43 (0)1 513 6407
rhorns.com

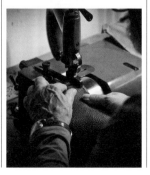

③
Saint Charles Apothecary, Mariahilf (6th)
Potions and lotions

Alexander Ehrmann's family have been pharmacists for six generations, so it was only natural that he'd launch his own apothecary. In 2006 he opened this business in a former chemist dating from 1886. Today the ornate 19th-century wooden shelving is stocked with herbal remedies homemade from healing plants grown on Ehrmann's farm.

What's not used in his immune-boosting capsules, soaps or comforting teas is chopped up and served in Ehrmann's neighbouring eight-seat restaurant Alimentary, or transformed into deliciously scented cosmetics sold in the branch across the road. "Healing herbs are the red thread that guides my business," says Ehrmann, who's always looking for new ingredients to use in his products.
30 Gumpendorfer Strasse, 1060
+43 (0)1 586 1363
saint.info

④
Loden Plankl, Innere Stadt (1st)
Top-notch traditional garb

This family-run traditional clothing specialist has been a sartorial ambassador for all things Austrian since it opened in 1830. Its wares include a vast array of loden coats made from the heavy waterproof wool that is the country's best-known textile export.

Whether you're looking to dress like a Von Trapp or just find an impeccably tailored goat-suede jacket, this is the place. Rifle the shelves of the chalet-style shop and discover a wide range of clothing, slippers, knitwear and beautiful, hand-embroidered childrenswear.
6 Michaelerplatz, 1010
+43 (0)1 533 8032
loden-plankl.at

⑤
Ludwig Reiter, Innere Stadt (1st)
Family-run footwear firm

Fourth-generation shoemakers and brothers Lukas, Till and Uz Reiter oversee the production of about 30,000 pairs of shoes a year. Their Ludwig Reiter range, distributed to some 200 outlets around the world, runs from dapper brogues to slip-on shoes for both men and women plus bags, briefcases and smaller leather accessories.

The company now operates four premises across the city but every piece they sell is still painstakingly crafted in Reiter's renovated farm complex on the outskirts of Vienna.
6 Führichgasse, 1010
+43 (0)1 512 6146
ludwig-reiter.com

⑥
Heldwein Jewellers, Innere Stadt (1st)
Bespoke jewellery

Jeweller, gemologist and goldsmith Anton Heldwein (*pictured*) combines the tradition of his family's company, which was founded in 1902, with a distinctly contemporary aesthetic. Craftsmen working in the brand's onsite workshop collaborate with customers to create elaborate and inspiring one-off pieces or simply to repair beloved and long-held objects. The shop also has a gallery featuring jewellery, silverware and tableware from the likes of Georg Jensen and Robbe & Berking.

If you're inspired by the collection you may want to book a consultation with Herr Heldwein himself, either to commission bespoke handmade pieces or just ask the maestro's advice on updating and adorning an existing item of jewellery.
13 Graben, 1010
+43 (0)1 512 5781
heldwein.at

⑦
Gegenbauer, Favoriten (10th)
Fluid assets

Erwin Gegenbauer's father founded this vinegar brewery in 1929; today the 10th-district premises also makes beer and olive oil, and is home to a shop. It's a bit of a ride from the city centre but is worth a visit – you can take a guided tour to learn more about the brewing and production processes and taste-test the range of pressed oil, balsamic vinegar, fruit juice, cider, wine and beer. Coffee lovers will enjoy the Gegenbauer espresso with a drop of vinegar. Gegenbauer also has a stall at Naschmarkt (stand 111).
3 Waldgasse, 1100
+43 604 1088
gegenbauer.at

⑧
Mühlbauer, Innere Stadt (1st)
Extensive headware range

Pop in to this Seilergasse shop to see the creations of a masterful milliner. Each hat is painstakingly made in the company's atelier on nearby Schwedenplatz, employing the same techniques used by Mühlbauer since it was founded in 1903. The affable Klaus Mühlbauer stresses quality and provenance above all. With everything from hunting-inspired hackensacks and fedoras to merino-wool flat caps and rabbit-fur headwarmers, there's a hat to suit all tastes and head sizes.
10 Seilergasse, 1010
+43 (0)1 533 5269
muehlbauer.at

⑨
Esbjerg, Innere Stadt (1st)
Bountiful beauty products

For more than 25 years Esbjerg has been one of the leading brands in high-end shaving and personal care products. Located on Krugerstrasse, one of Vienna's *einkaufsstrasse* (shopping streets), the pastel-pretty shop stocks candles, natural soaps, cosmetic creams, shampoos and fragrances from renowned brands such as Mühle, Heyland & Whittle and Penhaligons. Esbjerg also recently launched its own natural cosmetic line for both women and men; products include olive-infused anti-ageing serum and grapefruit-scent aftershave.
7 Krugerstrasse, 1010
+43 (0)1 513 1936
esbjerg.com

(10)
Herzilein Wien, Innere Stadt (1st)
Playful childrenswear

When former primary-school teacher Sonja Völker started designing and making clothes for her two children, little did she know that her homespun talent would translate into a profitable business. More than 10 years later, Völker now has three Herzilein shops in Vienna selling her own creations alongside a carefully chosen selection of toys and clothes by other brands.

Herzilein Wien is known for its bold and bright kidswear and signature prints. Other popular items include felt backpacks, and towels and blankets that can be customised with decorative embroidery and a child's name. Best of all, entering the puckish, colourful shop on Wollzeile is akin to stepping into an Enid Blyton book.
17 Wollzeile, 1010
+43 676 657 7106
herzilein-wien.at

22,50

(11)
Altmann & Kühne, Innere Stadt (1st)
Heritage chocolatier

Step into the yesteryear world of Altmann & Kühne where people queue up for tiny chocolate bonbons. The shop was designed by architect Josef Hoffmann and has been preserved in its original state. It's a fitting showcase for the beautiful chocolates that have been made by hand by the company since 1930. The house speciality is the Grillage, a chocolate cube with almonds. The charm continues when you leave too: purchased treats are packed in colourful boxes designed by the Wiener Werkstätte production group.
30 Am Graben, 1010
+43 (0)1 533 0927
altmann-kuehne.at

I was so busy shopping I forgot to buy tobacco…

(12)
Julius Meinl am Graben, Innere Stadt (1st)
Iconic gourmet-food purveyor

There isn't a single Austrian who wouldn't recognise the famous Moor logo of Julius Meinl. The history of this gourmet emporium dates back to 1862 when founder Julius Meinl started to sell pre-roasted coffee. The flagship Graben store is its most famous and stocks more than 17,000 delicacies from around the world.

Despite its vast inventory, the store painstakingly sources small specialist producers and rare delicacies. Try the poppy-seed cake from the Waldviertel region or venison sausage from Arlberg.
19 Graben, 1010
+43 (0)1 532 3334
meinlamgraben.at

Three more specialist shops

01 Staud's Wien, Ottakring:
The bustling Brunnenmarkt is home to Staud's Wien, one of Austria's oldest preserve producers. The family-run business started out as a fruit and vegetable wholesaler in 1883 and entered the jam market in the 1970s. It has since produced 95 varieties of jams and marmalades alongside compotes and chutneys. Other flavours include sour cherry and elderflower, plum and apple. The fruits are all sourced locally, whether it's apricots from the Venusberg Garden in the Danube Valley or white peaches from Burgenland. The shop also sells fresh fruit and vegetables, and baked goods and meat from Johann Winter; everything required for a well-stocked breakfast table.
stauds.com

02 Chronothek, Innere Stadt: Chronothek has an exceptional range of antique, vintage and modern timepieces, including limited-edition Patek Philippe, Franck Muller and Rolex watches. In the workshop, master watchmakers meticulously check and refurbish each piece.
chronothek.at

03 Vello Bike, Landstrasse: Bulgarian-born product designer Valentin Vodev has won numerous accolades for his cycle designs, including the prestigious Red Dot award for the Vello Speedster. The three Vello Bike models are made in Europe using quality materials.
vello.bike

VORSICHT! NICHT BERÜHREN!

⑬ Augarten, Leopoldstadt (2nd)
Fine ceramics

Augarten was founded in 1718 and is one of Europe's oldest porcelain manufacturers. And like many of the city's centuries-old makers, it has found the going a little tough in the past few decades. But an injection of new blood is helping to revive its fortunes. Augarten has recently expanded its heavily classicist and Jugendstil-oriented style by notching up some bold new collaborations, notably with design collective Mostlikely and speaker-maker MoSound. The company has a museum and shop alongside the factory within Palais Augarten.
1 Obere Augartenstrasse, 1020
+43 (0)1 2112 4200
augarten.at

Past master
——
Augarten has made ceramics for about 300 years

Hartmann, Innere Stadt (1st)
Spectacles made with love

This shop, founded by husband-and-wife team Erich and Ingrid Hartmann more than 30 years ago, specialises in custom buffalo and ox horn-rimmed spectacles. Each pair takes up to eight hours to meticulously hand-craft in an atelier on the outskirts of Vienna. Step into the cosy wood-panelled shop (formerly a century-old comb manufacturer) and get measured up. Expect a three to four-week wait for delivery, although impatient types can choose from prêt-à-porter styles or pick up other horn accessories, including combs and jewellery.
8 Singerstrasse, 1010
+43 (0)1 512 1489
hartmann-wien.at

15
Carissimo Letterpress,
Meidling (12th)
Putting their stamp on it

This wondrous workshop is located not far from Schönbrunn Palace. You'll find vintage printing presses as well as cards and paper in all shapes and shades. "Working with antique printing presses is a bit like reliving times gone by," says co-founder Ana Kaan. "Ours are old ladies by now." Her German press Maria Addolorata is a case in point: it survived both world wars and still produces the brand's greeting cards, notebooks, posters and custom-made paper products.
34-36 Singrienergasse, 1120
+43 650 888 5808
carissimo-letterpress.com

Clothing
Viennese threads

Gino Venturini, Innere Stadt (1st)
Finely crafted shirts

Gino Venturini and his son Nici create shirts that are masterful and timeless. Clients are measured up in the 1st-district shop that is manned by the duo and piled high with cufflinks, braces and formal accessories. The shirts have mother-of-pearl buttons and are made by a tailoring process that involves cutting every piece by hand.

The attention to detail, quality and design that goes into each shirt has seen the brand forge a reputation as a leading maker in a city that is known for its exceptional craftsmanship.
9 Spiegelgasse, 1010
+43 (0)1 512 8845
venturini.at

Fit for a king
—
Knize has clothed royals since the 1800s

KNIZE
NEW YORK · PARIS · BAD GASTEIN

I'm off to Knize to be measured for some trousers!

② Knize, Innere Stadt (1st)
Top tailoring

Vienna has been the unsung hero of bespoke sartorial style for centuries. Knize has clothed Austrian, Swedish and Spanish royalty since the 19th century, when Czech master tailor Josef Knize founded the firm. Its made-to-measure suits have a one-year waiting list so if you're looking for more instant gratification, explore the Adolf Loos-designed shop and pick up ready-to-wear items. It also stocks pieces by brands such as Tod's, Brioni, Lock & Co and Swaine Adeney Brigg, along with womenswear.
13 Graben, 1010
+43 (0)1 512 2119
knize.at

◐

Dantendorfer, Innere Stadt (1st)
Family man

Roy Dantendorfer has built his family business into a string of fashion shops that offer high-end pieces from independent designers such as Tory Burch from the US, 45rpm from Japan, Italy's Incotex, Germany's Odeeh and the UK's Harris Wharf. Dantendorfer was founded in 1948 in Salzburg by Roy's parents, who initially sold clothing alongside sports equipment. Roy took over 30 years ago and honed the focus to fashion. Tucked into an elegant, winding street in the 1st district, the Vienna shop reopened in August 2015 after an airy expansion by architect Scott Ritter.
9 Weihburggasse, 1010
+43 (0)1 512 5965
dantendorfer.at

③
Gebrüder Stitch, Neubau (7th)
Jean genes

We've all heard of bespoke suits and made-to-measure shoes – but how about applying that approach to jeans? In 2010, Moriz Piffl-Percevic and Mike Lanner decided to give up their branding jobs and pick up a needle and thread. With a budget of €10,000 they took a six-month tailoring course and began making cotton-wool jeans. Today the duo run shops in Vienna and Berlin. You can select your preferred style, cut, colour of yarn and fabric while sipping a glass of prosecco, and within four weeks your handmade jeans are ready to take home.
4 Mariahilfer Strasse, 1070
+43 680 144 9385
gebruederstitch.at

The right fit
The jeans are made using organic cotton

⑤
Kayiko, Mariahilf (6th)
Unconventional fashion

Karin Oèbster's avant garde menswear and womenswear is characterised by minimalist silhouettes, unconventional cuts and lots of folds, layers and draping. "I began with the classic kimono that fits everyone," says Oèbster of her clothes, which bear a strong Japanese aesthetic.

The mostly monochromatic pieces are displayed in a minimalist, whitewashed shop that's slightly out of the way in the 6th district. The clothing is made upstairs in the atelier by hand; the loose pantsuits, dresses and sculptural jackets are often one-of-a-kind.

"Anything can inspire me," says Oèbster. "It can be a track of music or even a ventilation grille; everyday things suddenly lead to a whole collection."
16 Windmühlgasse, 1060
+43 (0)1 585 4642
kayiko.com

I'm really more conservative than avant garde...

⑥
S/GHT, Neubau (7th)
Showcasing new talent

This womenswear shop has a personal approach to service – the friendly half-Japanese, half-Austrian founder Vivien Sakura Brandl (*pictured*) can often be found behind the till in her signature black specs. She is passionate about her selection of clothes and accessories, explaining that she seeks out "small young brands that are produced in Europe with quirky cuts".

This shop stocks more than 20 labels with a line-up of lesser-known designers, including silk dresses from Austrian Claudia Brandmair and knitted gloves from Mija t rosa.
24-25 Kirchengasse, 1070
+43 699 1225 6205
sight.at

⑦
Song, Leopoldstadt (2nd)
Hidden gem

"I wanted to hide a bit, the centre of town was becoming too commercial," says South Korea native Myung il Song, who moved her concept shop away from the first district to this quiet stretch of the Praterstrasse in 2006. Art, furniture, fashion and design are all under one roof here; drawers contain sparkling jewellery and covert corners hold collections by hard-to-find designers such as Paul Harnden. There are also exclusive collaborations with Lobmeyr and Lock & Co hatters, and Song's own furniture line.
11-13 Praterstrasse, 1020
+43 (0)1 532 2858
song.at

⑧
Lena Hoschek, Neubau (7th)
Retro chic

Designer Lena Hoschek makes traditional Austrian dirndls and 1950s-style dresses, skirts and blouses with Marilyn Monroe-style hourglass silhouettes. Hoschek set up her eponymous label in 2005 in her hometown of Graz, after a year-long internship at Vivienne Westwood's studio in London, and has since gone international with outposts in Germany, Italy, Switzerland and the US. The brand's flagship Vienna store is tucked away in the historic Spittelberg neighbourhood just behind the Museumsquartier.
To get a deeper understanding of Hoschek's luxurious materials and traditional workmanship, be sure to pop by her atelier in the 12th district (you'll need to make an appointment to do so).
Shop: 17 Gutenberggasse, 1070
+43 (0)1 5030 9200
Atelier: 27 Längenfeldgasse, 1120
+43 (0)1 5030 9100
shop.lenahoschek.com

⑨
Wubet, Leopoldstadt (2nd)
Globe-trotting accessories

Designer Arnold Haas (*pictured*) launched his accessories shop in 2010 on the up-and-coming Praterstrasse. The Claus Radler-designed showroom doubles as a gallery for emerging artists; the artwork complements Haas's alpaca-wool shawls, graphic silk scarves, hats and leather bags. His designs are inspired by his global travels in places such as Chile and Ethiopia. During his time in Africa for example, he picked up traditional beads and now turns them into necklaces. All textiles are woven by hand on antique looms.
11 Praterstrasse, 1020
+43 664 769 2102
wubet.com

I'm like
Arnold Haas:
shopping
around
the world
inspires me

Bookshops
Between the lines

①
Phil, Mariahilf (6th)
Lively prose

Christian Schädel launched bookshop-cum-café Phil in the 6th district between the Naschmarkt and Museumsquartier back in 2004. It offers a markedly different experience to most hushed bookstores. "It's a place where you can spend hours having breakfast, listening to music, flirting, getting drunk and, if you want, sleeping," he says. Schädel modelled Phil on the tea-slash-bookshops he experienced in Laos.

It feels like your very own living room, furnished with an eclectic collection of vintage chairs, tables and lamps that are as much for sale as the apple strudel and novels piled high on tables and shelves (you'll find everything from Austrian literature to English novellas and art publications). "It's a haven for those looking for a cosy place in the city for a sensual and intellectual retreat," says Schädel.
10-12 Gumpendorfer Strasse, 1060
+43 (0)1 581 0489
phil.info

②
Salon für Kunstbuch,
Neubau (7th)
Art titles and events

"I developed Salon für Kunstbuch in my studio as the life-size model of a bookshop," says Bernhard Cella, who has assembled 9,000 artists' books since its foundation in 2007. The collection of artworks and limited-edition books are arranged according to height and colour so that when you step inside the space, a shelf of bright red books will give way to Klein-blue titles, followed by snow-white manuscripts. The shop also hosts a series of thought-provoking events and readings.
11 Mondscheingasse, 1070
+43 660 445 7116
salon-fuer-kunstbuch.at

Things we'd buy
—— Perfect parting gifts

In recent years Austria has seen a return to in-house manufacturing and the capital is at the heart of this movement. Makers and venerated craftspeople are an indelible feature of the retail landscape here. So before bidding *auf wiedersehen* be sure to visit the ateliers, workrooms and shops to explore the best products Vienna has to offer. We recommend starting with a hat from milliner Mühlbauer and silverware by Wiener Silber Manufactur. Pick up some scarves from Wubet and a new pair of brogues from Ludwig Reiter. And don't depart without some treats from chocolatier Altmann & Kühne.

01 Hat by Mühlbauer
muehlbauer.at
02 Glassware by J & L Lobmeyr
lobmeyr.at
03 Saint Charles Apothecary tea
saint-charles.eu
04 Menswear by Gino Venturini
venturini.at
05 Hot chocolate and
wafers from Julius Meinl
meinlamgraben.at
06 Altmann & Kühne chocolates
altmann-kuehne.at
07 Wiesbauer sausage
wiesbauer.at
08 Staud's Wein jams
stauds.com
09 Books from Mak Museum
makdesignshop.at
10 Silverware by Wiener
Silber Manufactur
wienersilbermanufactur.com
11 Ceramics by Feinedinge
feinedinge.at
12 Weingut Wieninger wine
from Vinothek St Stephan
vinothek1.at
13 Enamelware by Riess *riess.at*
14 Soaps by Lederhaas
lederhaas-cosmetics.com
15 Zur Schwäbischen
Jungfrau doll
schwaebische-jungfrau.at
16 Shoes by Rosa Mosa
rosamosa.com
17 Shoes by Ludwig Reiter
ludwig-reiter.com
18 Scarves by Wubet *wubet.com*

01 Leather bags by R Horn's
rhorns.com
02 Saint Charles Apothecary
home remedy
saint-charles.eu
03 Male cosmetics by Esbjerg
esbjerg.com
04 Haircare by Less is More
lessismore.at
05 Cosmetics by Lederhaas
lederhaas-cosmetics.com

06 Carissimo Letterpress stationery
carissimo-letterpress.com
07 Womenswear by Natures
of Conflict
naturesofconflict.com
08 Hair and beard brushes
by Esbjerg *esbjerg.com*
09 Shoecare kit and polishes
by Scheer *scheer.at*

12 essays
—— Voices from Vienna

1
Rise and fall
Viennese history in a nutshell
by Joseph Pearson,
writer

2
West meets East
The city's cultural influences
by Marie-Sophie Schwarzer,
Monocle writer and
researcher

3
Space to create
An artist's legacy
by Alexei Korolyov,
writer

4
Hitting the right notes
A musical capital
by Armin Thurnher,
publisher

5
Wein from Wien
Austrian viticulture
by Vea Kaiser,
author

6
Constructing the bean
Coffeehouse design
by Gregor Eichinger,
architect

7
Pass it on
Hand-me-down heritage
by Lilli Hollein,
director of Vienna
Design Week

8
Grave matters
Viennese death obsession
by Markus Huber,
writer

9
Working titles
What's in a name?
by Josh Fehnert,
Monocle Edits editor

10
Spy hub
At your secret service
by Dardis McNamee,
writer

11
One step ahead
The rise of Wien cuisine
by Petra Percher,
writer

12
Art and soul
Shaking up schooling
by Kimberly Bradley,
Monocle Vienna
correspondent

*Ooh, the
essays
section
– time to
refresh
my drink*

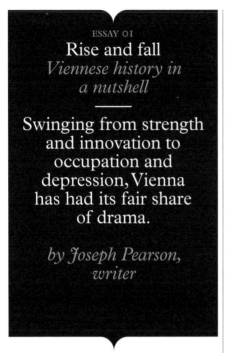

ESSAY 01
Rise and fall
Viennese history in a nutshell

Swinging from strength and innovation to occupation and depression, Vienna has had its fair share of drama.

by Joseph Pearson, writer

A brisk stroll around some of Vienna's most famous sites is all it takes to get a taste of the city's long and colourful history. Walking around the Hofburg, the imperial palace on Michaelerplatz, it's hard not to trip over the remains of the Roman military outpost, Vindobona (circa 15BC). The nearby streets still follow the contours of the old Roman walls.

Climbing the 343 dizzying steps of the tower of 14th-century St Stephen's Cathedral will help you acquaint yourself with medieval Vienna. This was an important time for the settlement, which had in the previous century not only obtained a city charter but also built a series of impressive walls, founded a

university and seen the rise of the Habsburg dynasty. There was also plenty of money, with the city's merchants trading down the Danube and south as far as Venice.

But with prosperity came an increased threat from the East: Vienna became famous, first in 1529 and then again in 1683, as a bulwark against Turkish invasions. The Ringstrasse (Ring Road) was once the site of fortifications that successfully and repeatedly held approaching armies at bay. Today this part of the city is an elegant network of open spaces, parks and palaces but throughout much of the 16th century it reverberated with the sound of intense fighting.

Although the city centre remained intact, the suburbs were ravaged by the conflicts and an intense period of rebuilding ensued. Many of the new buildings were in the Baroque style, such as the 1719 Chancellery building on Ballhausplatz, site of the Congress of Vienna held between 1814 and 1815 to provide a long-term peace plan for Europe in the wake of the Napoleonic Wars. The reactionary period, before the 1848 revolutions across the Austrian empire, was one of remarkable artistic flourishing: this was the shining era of Beethoven and Schubert, echoing the glory of the 18th-century Vienna enjoyed by Haydn and Mozart.

What would these composers have made of the explosion of cross-disciplinary talent at the dawn of the 20th century? Vienna in 1900

Famous facial hair
—
01 **Franz Joseph I (died 1916)**
Emperor of Austria-Hungary:
bushy biker sideburns.
02 **Gustav Klimt (died 1918)**
Erotic symbolist painter:
mangy hobo beard.
03 **Adolf Loos (died 1933)**
Modern-design pioneer:
chevron moustache.

Of the 183,000 Jews who lived in the city only 2,000 survived.

The city was defeated in April 1945 and as much as a quarter of it was left in ruins. For the next decade Vienna, like Berlin, was divided into zones controlled by the victorious Allied powers. It became an intriguing frontier city, sitting next to the Iron Curtain, its streets supposedly full of spies.

Independent Austria, declared neutral, later boomed with aid from the Marshall Plan.

"Vienna in 1900 positively buzzed with the unveiling of Sigmund Freud's psychoanalysis theories"

positively buzzed with the unveiling of Sigmund Freud's psychoanalysis theories, lost itself in the fictional worlds of Arthur Schnitzler and marvelled at the art and architecture of the Jugendstil (art nouveau) movement. Luminaries met in Viennese coffeehouses and the city sat contentedly at the cosmopolitan centre of a multinational empire, Austria-Hungary, under the rule of Emperor Franz Joseph I.

But hard times were ahead. The Austrian republic emerged from the First World War defeated and starved. It was a shadow of its imperial self. Nicknamed "Red Vienna", the city became a vanguard of social democracy in the 1920s but descended into fascism during the following decade. Austria is sometimes referred to as Germany's "first victim", but the Viennese welcomed Hitler's annexation in March 1938. Take a ride on the great wheel, or Riesenrad, in the Prater park, to see the darker side of Vienna's 20th century. The wheel is just one example of stolen property; the former Jewish owner, Eduard Steiner, was killed in Auschwitz.

It also internationalised. In 1979 the Vienna International Centre was built on the banks of the Danube. Here you will find the UN Headquarters. The end of the Cold War changed Vienna's position in Europe once again. Austria acceded to the EU in 1995. The Union joined it politically to its former possessions in east-central Europe. Vienna – a capital that had fluctuated between innovation, intolerance, imperial power and backwater blues – once again finds itself at the centre of Europe and marvelling at its newfound importance. — (M)

ABOUT THE WRITER: Joseph Pearson has a history doctorate from Cambridge, is the voice of *The Needle* blog and author of *Cityscopes Berlin*. He jeopardises his academic career with too much waltzing and *sekt* (sparkling wine).

ESSAY 02

West meets East
The city's cultural influences

The Habsburg empire only survived so long by embracing its diversity. Today its legacy lives on in the cultural pick'n'mix that makes Vienna such a sweet prospect.

by Marie-Sophie Schwarzer, Monocle writer and researcher

Arriving in Vienna, with its cobbled streets, grand boulevards and historic coffeehouses, can feel like a homecoming. Even if it's your first visit, there's something about this city that seems comforting and familiar.

It's no surprise that most people believe they know New York like the back of their hand because every street corner has featured in one film or another; London feels instantly familiar thanks to the novels of Charles Dickens and his compatriots, and the charm of Paris has been immortalised by the impressionists. With Vienna it's a different story. Sure, Carol Reed's *The Third Man* and Richard Linklater's *Before Sunrise* introduced the city to a wide audience but few places had so profound an impact on the culture and history of Europe as this city.

This is the place where schnitzel and strudel sit side by side on every corner-café menu; where Franz Schubert and Wolfgang Amadeus Mozart filled concert halls and where some 1,700 bridges crisscross its waterways (not even Venice can claim to have so many). It's no wonder that the imperial city reflects a fraction of every European town because – like its coffee – Vienna is a *melange*: a kaleidoscope of cultures and people that sits like a bridge between central and eastern Europe.

The city that originated as a Celtic settlement and later became the heart of the influential Austro-Hungarian empire has long been at the nucleus of European history. Its central geographic position played a part: it's a mere 50km hop to Slovakia, 200km to Hungary and 250km to the gilded towers of Prague. This proximity to other nations has helped make Vienna the cosmopolitan capital it is today.

As early as the 1900s the city made a name for itself as one of Europe's largest, with a population of close to two million. Even after its empire fell in the wake of the First World War, Vienna remained a haven for its neighbours. And every influx of people from different backgrounds contributed to the evolution of the city's culture and cuisine – *germknödel*, anyone?

The tide turned during the Second World War when the country became a hostile home and during the Cold War, Vienna lost its familiar central position, finding itself instead at the edge of western Europe on the frontier with the Soviet Bloc. But the drawing back of the Iron Curtain in 1989 reinstated the city as a unifying force and a magnet for

---

Three of Vienna's adpoted greats

---

01 Ludwig van Beethoven
Bonn-born composer.
02 The Empress Elisabeth of Austria
'Sissi' hailed from Munich.
03 Sigmund Freud
The psychoanalysist was born in the Czech Republic.

immigrants from all corners of the continent. In fact, immigration has been the driver behind its 10 per cent population growth in recent years.

Statistics aren't everything, of course, and Vienna retains a welcoming, villagey feel. But just how international the city is becomes apparent when you crunch the numbers: about 50 per cent of the population have foreign roots; 24 per cent are non-Austrian passport holders; and 32 per cent were born abroad. Assimilation is reflected in the lifestyle and identity of Vienna; the city symbolises the amalgamation of Europe's best features. It's one of the reasons it remains a desired destination for refugees seeking sanctuary from more dangerous – or simply less tolerant – places.

"Like its coffee, Vienna is a melange: a kaleidoscope of cultures and people"

It's only been a quarter of a century since Europe's dividing wall came down and Vienna regained its role as the place where east becomes west and vice versa. Newfound Europe-wide freedoms are at the root of the city's modern rebirth but with liberty comes vulnerability and when mass population movements begin, as in 2015, it's tempting for many nations to resort to putting up those barriers once more. Yet at the end of the day it's good to remember that Vienna wouldn't be the same today if immigrants such as Sigmund Freud and Gustav Mahler hadn't called it home at one point or another – and played a part in making it the cultural and intellectual engine of a continent. — (M)

ABOUT THE WRITER: MONOCLE's Marie-Sophie Schwarzer grew up in Germany. Numerous reporting trips have taken her to Vienna, where she likes to spend her afternoons roaming the Museumsquartier before feasting on platefuls of *kaiserschmarrn* at the nearest conveniently appointed *kaffeehaus*.

ESSAY 03
Space to create
An artist's legacy

No architect has laid such a unique stamp on Vienna as Freidensreich Hundertwasser, proto-hippie organicist and radical nature-lover.

by Alexei Korolyov, writer

When asked by Viennese friends what I like most about their city, I tend to say architecture or art, or else, more vaguely, "culture". When friends and family back home in Moscow pose that same question my reply, typically, is "freedom".

This notion will likely sound hollow to the Viennese – Austrian life can be morbidly codified and regimented, and active change is often strongly discouraged – yet there is something about Vienna that has inspired generations of creative minds: the Austrian capital has never (except perhaps briefly during the period of Nazi rule in the Second World War) really dictated any official prescription for art in the way that other cities have.

**Hundertwasser
must-sees**
—
01 **District heating plant**
Spittelau, Vienna.
02 **St Barbara Church**
Bärnbach, southern Austria.
03 **Hot spa resort
Rogner Bad Blumau**
Southern Austria.

And so while it may appear overly sedate and imperious in its Baroque and classicist grandeur, Vienna's true nature lies in experimentation.

Countless artists have taken advantage of this historically open attitude to art: that most famous artistic group, the brilliant cohort of Gustav Klimt's Secession, shocked its contemporaries with its sheer ambition and decadence and so too, almost a century later, did the unconventional creations of Friedensreich Hundertwasser.

Born into a poor Jewish family in 1928, Hundertwasser first gained prominence in the 1950s and had his reputation firmly established by the end of the following decade. He was prolific in many art forms, including painting, design and happenings. But it was his experiments in architecture that brought him the most fame.

An advocate of natural, organic forms, Hundertwasser believed that human habitat should be closer to nature – literally. His designs included vegetation on rooftops and fantastical apartment blocks with patchworked, customisable façades,

the idea being that any person should be able to reach out of their window and change the masonry around it at will. His naturist (in both senses of the word) views also found expression in his famous "Naked Speech" performance that he delivered in the nude in 1968 and the "Los von Loos" ("Away from Loos") manifesto, in which he went to war with the rationalism of Adolf Loos, another experimentalist architect, who declared that all ornament was "a crime".

Impractical and eccentric as all this sounds, Hundertwasser's vision became a reality in Vienna in 1985 when, at the behest of the then chancellor Bruno Kreisky and with the help of architect Josef Krawina, he completed what is now duly considered one of his greatest masterpieces: the Hundertwasserhaus. A communal residential block in the city's 3rd district, the building's multiple façades do not contain a single straight line (in a hyperbolic statement rivalling that of Loos' denouncement of ornamentation, Hundertwasser famously proclaimed straight lines "godless" and "a true tool of the Devil"). It is a riotous pastiche of colours, motifs and forms – a drunken hybrid of Tolkien's bucolic Shire

"There is something about Vienna that has inspired generations of creative minds"

and L Frank Baum's *The Wonderful Wizard of Oz.* To compound the whimsical impression, parts of the building are covered in leaves and grass, with shrubs and trees growing on rooftops and even escaping from individual apartments. Its floors – much like the floors at the nearby Kunst Haus Wien museum, another Hundertwasser creation that houses the world's only permanent collection of his works – are at best slightly tilting, at worst undulating like hobbit hills. "An uneven and animated floor is the recovery of man's mental equilibrium," Hundertwasser suggested. I wonder if the residents agree.

Health and safety risks aside, this building – standing defiantly amid its drab, grey council-flat surroundings – is evidence of Vienna's quirkier side (you need but look). And this is what I'm talking about when I say that I admire the city's "freedom". In many places, not least in my native Moscow, that word is often taken to mean licence to degrade and destroy. But in Vienna it means the right to invent and create, no strings attached. And that's what I mean by culture. — (M)

ABOUT THE WRITER: Alexei Korolyov moved to Vienna in 2012 and has been a contributor to various Monocle 24 shows and MONOCLE magazine ever since. He sometimes regrets the fact he studied literature, not architecture.

ESSAY 04

Hitting the right notes
A musical capital

———

While the city's musical heritage is deep, there's more to the sound of Vienna than Strauss and Mahler. Electronica is a key export, jazz fuses with Wienerlied, atonalism was born here and, always, there is opera.

by Armin Thurnher, publisher

Vienna is the music capital of the world. But what makes it worthy of such a claim? On the first day of January, Austria welcomes the new year with a waltz: "The Blue Danube" by Johann Strauss II – the nation's unofficial national anthem – is played by the Vienna Philharmonic Orchestra in the Golden Hall of the Wiener Musikverein and broadcast live to some 50 million people around the world. The lucky few to win a seat in the annual raffle sway blissfully under the chandeliers while at home music aficionados cluster around their radios and televisions making resolutions to visit Vienna. Forget fireworks: this is the only way to start a new year.

A true music capital should have an impressive roster of historical musical residents and Vienna excels on that front. Schubert was born here and maestros from Beethoven to Brahms, Mozart to Mahler – not to mention Schönberg, Webern, Berg and Krenek – all lived in the city at one time or another. Countless classical pieces premiered in the salons of the Viennese aristocracy and on the stages of the city's public theatres. Many of Beethoven's symphonies were first performed at the Theater an der Wien, which from 1955 was used as a venue for musicals but has recently returned to its original purpose of staging operas.

Opera forms part of this city's soul. It was only in 1955 when the war-damaged Haus am Ring – as the Viennese are wont to affectionately call the State Opera – finally reopened, that the Second Austrian Republic considered itself complete. Today the institution is a symbol for the representative arts.

A music capital needs music festivals. Cue major annual events such as the Wiener Festwochen every May and June – the city's most prestigious festival with guest performances and local productions – and Wien Modern, an important festival for contemporary music every October and November. It also requires homegrown orchestras and ensembles. In addition to the Philharmonic Orchestra, Wiener Symphonikern, the Radio-Symphonieorchester and numerous smaller groups, the Klangforum Wien deserves special mention. It is arguably the world's best new music ensemble; when it is not touring it plays concerts in front of its home crowd at the Konzerthaus.

"A music capital should have an impressive roster of historical musical residents and Vienna excels on that front"

But Vienna's many music venues don't just reverberate with the sound of strings, brass and woodwind, and its events don't simply revolve around its famous historical stars: the pop scene is alive and kicking. Numerous German-speaking bands and solo artists have emerged over the last few years – notably, the band Wanda, who released their fun,

Vienna's music festivals

01 Donauinselfest
Eclectic open-air festival every June at Donauinsel.
02 Jazz Fest Wien
Each June and July, across various venues.
03 Rock in Vienna
Rock and metal festival every June at Donauinsel.

catchy debut album in 2014 and have taken Austria by storm.

The scene here is not afraid to experiment. Many artists seamlessly merge local tastes with international music traditions; the songs of Willi Resetarits and Ernst Molden are perfect examples of how rock, blues, jazz and *wiener musik* can be successfully fused. For wittier, keener and more contemporary examples of the Wienerlied (that traditional but popular genre of Vienese music often bordering on kitsch) one need only refer to the ditties of Trio Lepschi or Kollegium Kalksburg. Even Vienna's electronic artists have conquered the international scene – just think of DJ Patrick Pulsinger or the guitar riffs of Christian Fennesz.

Of course there is always room for improvement: there is sadly no venue for contemporary musical theatre and Vienna is arguably a victim of its own success; try and avoid the army of camera-wielding tourists that swarms around the golden statue of Johann Strauss II in the Stadtpark and poses in front of Mozart's Old Town residence. A music capital should appeal to the masses and there's no denying that Vienna is the ultimate crowd-pleaser. — (M)

ABOUT THE WRITER: Armin Thurnher is a journalist, publisher, chief editor of the weekly Viennese magazine *Falter* and author of numerous books.

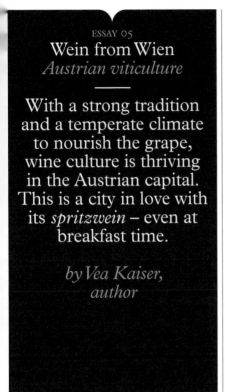

ESSAY 05
Wein from Wien
Austrian viticulture

——

With a strong tradition and a temperate climate to nourish the grape, wine culture is thriving in the Austrian capital. This is a city in love with its *spritzwein* – even at breakfast time.

*by Vea Kaiser,
author*

In other parts of the world it might be considered cause for concern if the mayor, after tough coalition talks, were to face the waiting press and announce the successful agreement with the words: "Fetch the *spritzwein*!" Not so in Vienna. When Michael Häupl's first official act, as the city's re-elected mayor, was to demand alcohol – and the most Viennese of alcohol at that (the *spritzwein* or *weisser* spritzer is a traditional mix of one part white wine to one part sparkling water) he firmly earned a place for himself in the hearts of the Viennese.

Elsewhere, a mayor with a roguish appreciation for wine might be viewed with suspicion. In Vienna he is admired, loved and respected – just as the Viennese admire, love and respect their wine. Vienna's terroir may not be the largest but it is the world's only wine-growing area located wholly within the municipality of a metropolis.

Some 190 producers cultivate vineyards across six districts. This is possible due to the city's unique geography: in the west the city huddles against the foothills of the Vienna Woods and the northeastern end of the Alps, that provide both sun-soaked slopes and shelter. The Danube Valley brings a cooling breeze and a combination of sand, loam and *muschelkalk* (limestone), providing the best possible soil for white wine.

The thriving wine culture is the legacy of Vienna's two greatest powers: the Romans and the Habsburgs, both of them passionate wine drinkers. While the Christians officially condemned everything of pagan origin, they not only maintained the viniculture introduced by Emperor Probus but increased it until the medieval city was ringed by vineyards. And it is thanks to a Habsburg that one of Vienna's greatest pleasures was first introduced. In 1784, Emperor Joseph II allowed Vienna's wine growers to serve wine straight from their vineyards, thus establishing *heurigen* (wine taverns). They have been flourishing ever since. For a limited period each year vineyards throw open their doors and serve their latest vintages with fresh, hand-made dishes, often with *wienerlied-spieler* (musicians) playing old folksongs on traditional instruments. I challenge you to find a cosier atmosphere anywhere else in Europe.

> *"It was only once I moved abroad that it dawned on me that in other parts of the world, daytime drinking is not the norm"*

There is only one reliable way to tell if a Viennese vineyard is *ausgesteckt* (open to the public and serving food and wine): if you spot a small green bush hanging in front of the entrance, you are welcome to walk in. Of course these days the opening hours are also often advertised online but this is the only contemporary touch to these otherwise 18th-century institutions. While many places now cater to fussy tourists with schnitzel made from chicken or beef and served with (sacrilege) fried potatoes or fried egg, in the *heurigen* convention prevails. They offer only authentic Viennese cuisine with traditionally prepared dishes.

But the *heurigen* are not the only venues where the Viennese like to indulge in wine: in the city centre you will find more wine bars than clubs, each offering splendid wines such as the so-called *schankweine* (unlabelled wines purchased by the landlords in two-litre bottles) at bargainous prices, and even the coffeehouses serve wine. Did you really think all those great writers, painters and composers drew their inspiration solely from coffee?

After the *melange*, the *weisser* spritzer is the classic coffeehouse drink. And don't be surprised if you see people ordering these before midday – "a spritz always fits", as they say. Admittedly, with its high content of sparkling water you need to drink a fair few to get properly sozzled but look out for the regulars who totter from one coffeehouse to another. I have to confess, it was only once I moved abroad that it dawned on me that in other parts of the world, daytime drinking is not the norm. Of course, the French enjoy a glass of wine with their lunch and who can imagine the British without their after-work pints, but in terms of quantity, the Viennese who start with a morning spritz

Vienna's most popular white wine varieties
—
01 Grüner veltliner
Crisp and aromatic.
02 Riesling
Ripe and flavourful.
03 Gemischter satz
Characterful and fruity.

beat them all. It doesn't help that an *achtel weiss* – in Vienna one never orders a "glass" of white or red wine but a *sechzehntel* (sixteenth), an *achtel* (eighth) or a *viertel* (quarter) – is always wickedly cheap. And why should it be otherwise when the wine is pressed on your very doorstep?

If you leave Vienna without enjoying a couple of *achtel weiss* in a wine tavern or a spritzer in a coffeehouse, you can't truly claim to have been to Vienna. Wine is as much a part of this city as schnitzel, the Wiener Riesenrad Ferris wheel and choirboys. — (M)

ESSAY 06
Constructing the bean
Coffeehouse design
————
Coffeehouses in the Austrian capital are seen as an extension of the living room and should strike the right balance between tradition and innovation. But above all they must reflect the people who visit them.

by Gregor Eichinger, architect

The coffeehouse concept only works in the city. In a village it would be too large, out of place – but in the city the coffeehouse is an expansion of public space, a communal living room. A Viennese coffeehouse in particular is not about eating or drinking but rather about lingering; *presence*. It's a space that's been put at the disposal of the people for them to simply be; it's a place to see and be seen, a zone in which one can act the host or enjoy being a guest.

I'm a Viennese architect and in 2011, I was the "coffeehouse expert" behind a two-part exhibition called *The Great Viennese Café: A Laboratory* at the Museum of Applied Art. Here we explored the idea of the coffeehouse as social hub and how that role is shifting as we move into the 21st century.

My affinity with coffeehouses and their design comes from my love for people. They are pure user interfaces, in contrast with hospitals or airports, say,

ABOUT THE WRITER: Vea Kaiser is a young Austrian author. Her debut novel, *Blasmusikpop*, was named the best German-language debut at the International Festival du Premier Roman in Chambéry and she was named author of the year in Austria in 2014.

that have other functional elements with which as a member of the public, you will never come into contact with. For an architect, coffeehouses are the real thing: undiluted, unfiltered, a double shot.

My work is tremendous fun but creating the perfect interface is a huge challenge that's easy to get wrong. I am constantly asking myself: should we preserve the Viennese coffeehouse or experiment with it?

First, preservation. Turning the coffeehouse into a kind of museum is a horrific idea; over-preservation is like enbalming or mummifying: it is stuffy and outdated. A coffeehouse should be the complete opposite of a museum. The only reason coffeehouses have survived for so long – including some of Vienna's most popular, such as Café Sperl (*see page 39*), which has been a hangout for intellectuals since 1880, or Café Central, where legend has it that Trotsky, Stalin and Hitler all spent time – is their universal appeal. That's alongside the high-quality materials and age-old rituals associated with them (Vienna's traditional coffeehouses often turned a fancy profit, allowing them to invest in ornamental carved wood and customised interiors).

These things will still resonate in 5,000 years. But in their early years even historical coffeehouses were continually updated; they followed the newest fashions and trends, were recast every five or six years and filled with modern furnishings. Back then, no one wanted to stand still.

Then there's experimentation. The designer of a coffeehouse has to take modern conditions into consideration. Today Vienna's coffeehouses suffer from high rents, consumption tax and sizeable staff costs, so endlessly updating tradition doesn't make sense. But we can redefine the coffeehouse, recognising the fact that we are in the midst of major social developments.

Think about it: the connections and interactions that now exist electronically through social media are the connections and interactions that once played out in the coffeehouse – just without the coffee and *kipferl* (croissants). Through careful design, we can create a space where these relationships and experiences can blossom once again.

> *"I am constantly asking myself – should we preserve the Viennese coffeehouse or experiment with it?"*

The Viennese will always treasure their favourite old hangouts; new cafés trying to imitate the institutions will simply insult their intelligence. New coffeehouses – such as Café Ansari (*see page 36*) on Praterstrasse, which I designed in 2012 – have to keep contemporary culture in mind, without resorting to cookie-cutter concepts used by the big coffee chains. Designing the coffeehouse of the future means remembering communication as well as contemplation means offering a contemporary version of the escapism and subtle exhibitionism that have drawn dreamers and doers into Vienna's coffeehouses for centuries. — (M)

ABOUT THE WRITER: Gregor Eichinger is an architect and designer. He runs his own studio, Eichinger Offices, and teaches at the Academy of Fine Arts in Munich and the University of Applied Arts Vienna. He has designed numerous coffeehouses across the city.

ESSAY 07
Pass it on
Hand-me-down heritage

——

Amid slow but steady gentrification and the advent of international brands, how can Vienna keep hold of its traditions?

by Lilli Hollein, director of Vienna Design Week

Yesterday at my aunt's dinner table, conversation turned to a specifically Viennese tradition scrupulously upheld in my family: the inheritance of apartment leases from one generation to the next.

My aunt has lived in the same apartment almost all her life; she and my mother grew up there in the 1950s. It's a fantastic space with magnificent stucco ceilings, tiled stoves and so much room. At one time it was home to 10 people; today just two people live there.

I've been keeping up the family tradition too. Together with my husband and my daughter I live in the apartment in which I spent my childhood and where my father spent his. Since 1942, various generations of the Hollein family have been renting this 280 sq m property in one of the most popular districts of the city.

The two apartments in which my parents grew up are just a few streets from each other and, as I explain to the American neighbour who has joined us for dinner how much the area has changed in the past 80 years, I realise how many incredible stories took place within the space of a few blocks.

There was Victor Gruen, inventor of the shopping mall, who lived on the corner of the alley before he emigrated to the US; the Palais Schwarzenberg, a wonderful Baroque palace that we at Vienna Design Week have used as a venue for the festival, sits directly opposite us. And two blocks further down is the apartment where modernist architect Richard Neutra spent his last years after returning from the US. This was also the area in which the Palais Rothschild stood before it was torn down in 1954 two blocks further up, more recent history manifests itself in G-Stone Recordings and Richard Dorfmeister's (AKA Kruder & Dorfmeister) studios. In the late 1990s *The K & D Sessions* album

> *"Just as Viennese apartments are passed from one generation to another, so too are Viennese professions"*

seemed to be playing in every club, shop and bar from Vienna to Tokyo. In just six blocks, a cross-section of this country's culture and history unfolds.

Just as Viennese apartments are passed from one generation to another, so too are Viennese professions – although as in many European cities, this tradition is now at risk. Due to rising rents, gentrification is slowly changing the city's texture: small, specialised businesses with Austrian chains of production are being replaced by big international brands. The knowledge and experience that has been fostered over generations in these special places is in danger of being lost.

It was these designers and small manufacturers that Vienna Design Week had in mind when we introduced a scheme called Passionswege that connects contemporary designers with artisans from across the city to work on joint projects. It was our mission to create not just an awareness of these workshops and their wonderful atmospheres but

also to highlight the quality and expertise found within.

One company involved in the project was J&L Lobmeyr (*see page 52*), a glass and chandelier manufacturer founded in 1823 that has collaborated with some of Austria's greatest designers, including Adolf Loos and Josef Hoffmann. The champagne glasses by Oswald Haerdtl are quite stunning. I recommend that every visitor to Vienna make a trip to its showroom on Kärntnerstrasse.

Every year Vienna Design Week chooses a different neighbourhood to focus on and uncovers some of the city's hidden gems. Hornware manufacturer Petz in the 15th district is one such example. The workshop machines were made by the firm specifically for its own work and passed down to the current owner by his grandparents. Other specialist crafts range from brush-making to vinegar manufacture; Gegenbauer (*see page 57*), a vinegar producer in the 10th district, is another must-visit.

In Vienna, passing our homes down through the generations is part of our culture. Now we have to ensure we continue to do the same with our rich design tradition, so that these masters of their trades can pass on their hard-won skills to future generations. — (M)

ABOUT THE WRITER: Vienna native Lilli Hollein studied industrial design at the University of Applied Arts Vienna before she became a curator, founder and director of Vienna Design Week.

ESSAY 08
Grave matters
Viennese death obsession

From its popular central graveyard to upbeat funeral parades, Vienna has been fascinated by the macabre for centuries. Yet it's an interest that is taken with good humour – and visitor participation is encouraged.

by Markus Huber, writer

If you ever find yourself faced with having to explain Vienna to a foreigner, Seegasse could be a good place to start. This pokey little alley, a stone's throw from the historical centre, is home to Vienna's oldest graveyard, which now lies unceremoniously in the backyard of a residential building. A cemetery in a backyard? Wait until you find out that said residential building is actually an old people's home. A nursing home with integrated burial ground? Welcome to Vienna.

The Viennese are well known for their dark sense of humour and fascination with the macabre. If, like me, you have lived in Vienna long enough to feel Viennese, it's highly likely you no longer notice it. When you look at Vienna from an outsider's perspective however, death is omnipresent.

Nowhere else in the world will you find such a high concentration of (official and non-official) graveyards and few funeral parades match the Viennese in terms of pomp and circumstance. Not many cities list a graveyard as one of their top attractions but Vienna does and with just cause. The Zentralfriedhof (central cemetery) is indeed a unique place: in addition to some 330,000 graves it is also home to more magnificent buildings and art nouveau architecture than the average city. Plus its list of "residents" reads like an encyclopaedic catalogue of central European thought and culture.

"A nursing home with integrated burial ground? Welcome to Vienna"

Even in the city centre you will stumble across the dead, perhaps without realising. You will see the snakes of tourists queuing in front of the numerous Habsburg grave-chambers throughout the 1st district; you will stroll past churches where a multitude of church dignitaries are buried; you might even pass the so-called Fool's Tower (Narrenturm), a former mental asylum, that today houses a pathologic-anatomic collection. And even if you somehow manage to avoid all of these, there is no missing the glorious St Stephen's Cathedral: the entire basement is a hollow space, where the mortal remains of the Viennese were collected for centuries. Needless to say, it is also open to visitors.

The Funeral Museum in the Zentralfriedhof offers guided tours of Vienna's underworld and once a year, when businesses hold late-night opening hours, it invites visitors to test their collection of coffins. Traditionally it is the most popular event of the night.

Of course, many of these activities are aimed at tourists and don't in themselves prove the Viennese fascination with the macabre. But when it comes to giving a fitting send-off to their loved ones, the Viennese excel themselves. The Austrian phrase *scheenen leich* translates as "marvellous funeral"; guests are fully expected to enjoy themselves after the last rites.

This fascination with death has permeated all aspects of culture: try and think of a single Austrian musician who has never sung about death (you'll be hard pressed). The same goes for theatre, literature and even the fine arts. Death may be omnipresent but it is approached with humour and high spirits.

It's a subject that has also infiltrated the language: the Austrians have a multitude of ways to express that somebody is about to "pop their clogs" or "bite the dust". *Einen*

> **Buried in Vienna**
> ⸻
> **01 Franz Schubert**
> Short-lived but extremely prolific musician.
> **02 Maximilian I of Mexico**
> Only monarch of the Second Mexican empire.
> **03 Falco (Johann Hölzel)**
> Austrian rock musician and rapper.

abgang machen means "to make an exit", *die patschen strecken* is "to slip out of one's slippers" and the ever-so-playful *in den holzpyjama hüpfen* is "to jump into wooden pyjamas". Sweet dreams.

Many psychologists have tried to find an explanation for this morbid fascination. The findings are rather weak. One thing they can be sure of though is that it affects all walks of life: ever the romantic, Karl von Habsburg, grandson of the last Austrian emperor, took his girlfriend Francesca Thyssen to the vault of the Capuchin Church – where all his ancestors are buried – on a date. Once there he took her hand and didn't ask "Will you marry me?" but rather, "Would you like to be buried here?" She acquiesced. And is now Francesca von Habsburg. — (M)

ABOUT THE WRITER: **Markus Huber** has lived in Vienna since 1992. In 2004 he founded *Fleisch*, a quarterly magazine about lifestyle, culture and politics. He also writes a weekly column for the widest circulating Austrian weekly *News*. He's the funny guy.

Working titles
What's in a name?

——

'Magister', professor, 'doktor': titles matter here. The country may have moved on from its royalist history but the respect for academic achievement isn't a mark of entitlement.

*by Josh Fehnert,
Monocle Edits editor*

First-timers could be forgiven for finding Vienna stuffy or unapproachable. Its past is writ large in stately architecture, where visitors marvel open-mouthed at ornate palaces built by the many for the veneration of the few. But there's another revealing relic of the city's long-held obsession with status: a peculiar reverence for titles.

For the Viennese, email introductions, phone calls and even names supplied for dinner reservations are peppered or prefixed with words such as *magister* (someone holding a master's degree), *professor* or *doktor*. It's a curiously stiff manner of address. Onlookers may even reason that academic qualifications – in careers that don't involve preserving life or protecting the law – are almost wholly irrelevant the moment they are achieved or until a new job prospect looms.

This strange proclivity for academic appellation came under scrutiny as I sat in one of the city's famed cafés. "This way master," said a surly waiter to my companion, an affable Austrian-about-town with whom this server had fostered a long-running and good-natured patter. It was a cheerful chide – a subtle sublimation of the relationship between the waiter and the waited-on, and a revealing one too. I realised that the trait, which I had seen as outdated and austere, was ripe to be wryly undermined. But what does this vignette say about the city and where does this obsession with status come from?

Vienna's regal roots run deep. Austria was the centre of the Habsburg empire from the 1860s to the end of the First World War and successive emperors (some mad and moody, others benign) shaped it with the construction of a series of grand palaces, each in its way a statement of power, wealth and exclusivity. As a nexus of trade and the stomping ground of the elites within the Austro-Hungarian empire, class, breeding and refinement became everyday preoccupations among its population.

What people may not know is what happened next. During the early 20th century a socialist zeal overtook the city and an admirable crop of art deco constructions sprang up to acknowledge the city's proletarian turn. Social housing spiked and complexes such as the pinky-hued Karl Marx Hof building (*see page 114*) were erected. Likewise the 1,300-person capacity Amalienbad swimming pool (*see page 115*) is testament to the mood of solidarity, togetherness and public provision that grew in the wake of the fallen empire. The so-called Red Vienna era was here, healthcare and out-of-work provisions grew, architects such as Josef Hoffmann, Clemens Holzmeister and Adolf Loos flourished and shaped the city until Austria was annexed by Nazi Germany

> *"The Viennese are proud of their history but not bound by it"*

**Red Vienna
architectural gems**
—
01 Karl-Seitz-Hof (21st)
Designed by Hubert Gessner
and has 1,127 apartments.
02 Reumannhof (5th)
Ornately tiled complex.
**03 George-Washington-Hof
(10th)**
Includes an integrated library
and nursery.

in 1938. One kind-minded socialist remains. Vienna is still Europe's biggest landlord, provides cheap housing for residents and owns 25 per cent of homes here.

After the Second World War, as a frontier of the Iron Curtain, the city's identity was tested by waves of allied troops, espionage and uncertainty. As politics, borders and governments shifted during the 20th century, a respect for education, hard work and academic achievement held firm – and manifested in the Viennese respect for titles.

This all occurred to me as I sat in the Oswald Haerdtl-designed finery of the 1950s gem Café Prückel (*see page 38*). With a *melange* in hand it seemed a suitably democratic place to understand the interesting dichotomy at play. The Viennese are proud of their history but not bound by it. The city was built by royalty but isn't beholden to it. Here in one of its many coffee spots, diplomats sit next to *magisters* beside housewives and chattering children. Lingering is encouraged and service brisk – at times downright rude, regardless of your social standing. It's here that bolshie waiters wait in waistcoats to challenge the pomposity of the entitled, and where a true picture of the city comes for just the cost of a coffee. — (M)

ABOUT THE WRITER: MONOCLE's Edits editor Josh Fehnert oversaw a Vienna city survey for MONOCLE in 2015 (and spent more than a little time sipping coffee in Café Prückel due to the windy weather). He also developed a taste for *sturm*, a lightly alcoholic fermented grape juice, as an end-of-day sipper.

ESSAY 10

Spy hub
At your secret service
—

Nestled neatly between East and West and home to 1,700 foreign diplomats, Vienna has become a focal point for post-Cold War espionage sagas. Little wonder then that the film industry comes a-calling for its spy stories.

by Dardis McNamee, writer

On 9 July 2010, the press gathered at Vienna International Airport to await the exchange of 14 Russian and US intelligence agents. The two planes landed and taxied toward each other, stopping wing tip to wing tip, as the spies were ferried across in a black van. Within 90 minutes, the biggest swap in post-Cold War history was over.

But in Vienna the story was just beginning. For weeks, newspapers were filled with stories about "spy hub Vienna". It seemed they missed the romance of the old days, of codes and conspiracies, of moles, microfilm and MI6, and the forgotten 4th floor of the US embassy on Boltzmanngasse.

After all, for half a century, at the edge of the Iron Curtain, this charming central European city had been the setting for drama worthy of Hollywood. Assigned formal neutrality under the four-power occupation, it was a buffer zone between East and West. And while the Allies replaced their military commanders with diplomats in 1950, the Soviets retained a military presence in Vienna and Austria until 1955 – which helps explain the comfort Russia felt in using Vienna as the site for its swaps, dead drops and ongoing spy operations.

Today little has changed. As a UN headquarters city, Vienna is host to many international government monitoring bodies, including the Organization for Security and Cooperation in Europe, the International Atomic Energy Agency and the UN Office on Drugs and Crime, as well as some 17,000 diplomats – "about half of them with some connection to intelligence", says Siegfried Beer, founding director of the Austrian Center for Intelligence, Propaganda and Security Studies in Graz, making Austria the country with the highest density of foreign intelligence operatives in the world.

"Vienna is a city where people can withdraw," says Dr Karin Kneissl, international law professor and a former diplomat in the Austrian Ministry of Foreign Affairs. "It has discreet places, a nice quality of life, a calm atmosphere and exceptionally good flight connections."

Until recently, Austria also had a very strong banking secrecy policy. This enabled operatives to set up accounts without being asked a lot of questions and "facilitated the money transfer among groups involved in organised crime", says Kneissl.

Then came 1989. Gradually communist secret-police archives revealed Austrian public figures knee-deep in espionage activities. Helmut Zilk, ORF TV journalist and former mayor of Vienna, turned out to have been a paid informant for the Czechoslovak intelligence service between 1965 and 1968. And Otto Schulmeister, editor in chief of Austrian daily *Die Presse*, was on the payroll of the CIA from 1962 through to the 1970s.

Today Vienna still acts as the setting for Russian espionage activities. The Russian SVR maintains an intelligence network here. The 2009 assassination of Umar Israilov – a key witness in a case involving Chechnya's president Ramsan Kadyrov – on a Vienna street was attributed to the spy milieu, as was the attempted kidnapping of the head of Kazakhstan's National Security Committee in Vienna in 2008.

"This charming central European city had been the setting for drama worthy of Hollywood"

**Must-visits for
The Third Man fans**
—
01 Sewer Tour
Karlsplatz-Girardipark, 1010.
**02 Wiener Riesenrad
Ferris wheel**
Riesenradplatz, 1020.
03 Third Man Museum
25 Pressgasse 25, 1040.

But in the end it may simply be Vienna's cherishing, even cultivation, of its reputation as a spy hub that keeps the tradition alive. Legendary spy thriller *The Third Man*, with a screenplay by UK novelist (and former MI6 officer) Graham Greene, is still screened each week in Vienna, at the English-language Burg Kino, as it has been for some 30 years. In addition, several organisations host walking tours tracing the steps of Harry Lime, played by Orson Welles, through neighbourhoods and even the city sewers, almost unchanged since the film was released in 1949. — (M)

ABOUT THE WRITER: Dardis McNamee is the publisher and editor at large of *Metropole: Vienna* in English, a city magazine and online community. Former speechwriter for two US ambassadors to Austria, she is co-author of the 2011 Frommer's *Vienna and the Danube Valley*. She has lived in Vienna for 20 years.

ESSAY 11
One step ahead
The rise of Wien cuisine
—
Amid the rush to embrace international food fads, Vienna's unfussy traditional cuisine is enjoying a resurgence as a new generation discovers the joy of the 'wirtshaus'.

*by Petra Percher,
writer*

The Viennese love their jokes. Have you heard the one about the day of reckoning? "When the end of the world is nigh, go to Vienna. They are still 10 years behind the rest of us."

While there may be scraps of truth to this, when it comes to food at least, Vienna is ahead of the game. Vegan burger joints, street-food markets, paleo diets, third-wave coffeehouses, smoothie shops, smart cocktail bars: the city has seen its fair share of food crazes. But Vienna's most persistent trend – the *wirtshaus* (or more colloquially, *beisl*) – is not a concept imported from New York, London or Paris; these traditional Austrian taverns have been around for donkey's years. And importantly, they have learnt how to adapt.

Stefanie Herkner has a passion for all things vintage. Her restaurant Zur Herknerin (*see page 35*) is in a former plumbing supplies shop – the word *Installationen* (Plumbing) still marches across the façade in a blocky 1960s typeface – and is furnished with all manner of treasures from the nearby flea market. Herkner, the daughter of an innkeeper, serves simple soul food: aspic from the Slovenian farm of her grandparents, home-styled pickled herring, delicious *knödel* (dumplings) and a fruit jelly made from a well-guarded recipe belonging to her late father.

Zur Herknerin is just one example of how the recent *beisl*-boom – led by an army of idealists and self-taught gastronomes – has taken the city by storm. At the forefront of the trend is Christian Petz, a Michelin-starred chef who turned his back on the fine-dining scene to open his own *wirtshaus*, Petz im Gusshaus (*see page 32*) in the city's 4th district.

The original Gusshaus was a simple, no-frills space dominated by a large table and a curved bar where guests could drink and smoke, with a windowless, wood-panelled dining room beyond. The interior remains much the same but people seem to follow Petz wherever he goes. Those that do are rewarded with delectable examples of New Viennese cuisine: potato soup with smoked trout, green beans with breadcrumbs and chitterlings in riesling with vongole. The meals of many an Austrian childhood.

Viennese cuisine is a product of the imperial era, when recipes from Austria, Hungary, Bohemia, Moravia, upper Adria and the Balkans merged into what became known as the *wiener küche* – the only cuisine in the world named after a city.

> "*The Viennese have turned their back on over-complicated dishes and instead prefer to master old recipes*"

When it comes to fusion food at least, Vienna is certainly ahead of the times. Today this type of food is a huge part of the zeitgeist: the Viennese have turned their back on over-complicated dishes and instead prefer to master old recipes by trying to reduce the amount of meat they use and making the most of simple, seasonal and regional ingredients. And they are not afraid to shout about it: menus are now so crammed with information – from lists of suppliers to the names of the farm, the farmer or even the cow – that it sometimes becomes difficult to spot the actual dish among the stories of provenance.

In the early 20th century *wirtshäuser* started popping up all across the outskirts of Vienna, especially in the old working-class districts. But many of them subsequently closed, their atmosphere deemed too traditional and their food too greasy, too meaty and too offal-focused for the sushi generation. Only the rundown taverns renovated by ambitious young upstarts got a second chance.

The *wirtshaus* has always been a place to eat, drink, gossip, play cards and talk politics but in a city saturated with eating spots, new venues need to find fresh ways to bring in the punters. One young couple – a graphic designer and an electrician who now practises traditional Chinese medicine – have renovated and reinvented a traditional *wirtshaus* in the 20th district that opened its doors in 1901. Here, depending on your mood, you can now choose between rich minced-meat roasts and goulash or sourdough pancakes, readings and yoga sessions. As part of its image makeover the *beisl* was renamed Bin beim Art'ner, and the average age of its customers was swiftly reduced by half. Skopik + Lohn (*see page 33*) in the

---

Three more wirtshäuser

01 Das Eduard
1 Sparkassaplatz, 1150.
02 Zum Friedensrichter
57 Obere Donaustrasse, 1020.
03 Automat Welt
11 Volkert-platz, 1020.

hip Karmelitermarkt neighbourhood of the 2nd district, is a substitute living room for many Viennese. This carefully renovated *wirtshaus*, with elements borrowed from both US diners and Parisian brasseries, offers an unconventional mix: elegant waiters contrast with the energetic wall and ceiling graffiti by artist Otto Zitko and black pudding with horseradish purée sits on the menu next to classic steak-frites. Enigmatic innkeeper and co-founder Horst Scheuer is omnipresent: his irrepressible drive for perfection is the key to the success of this *wirtshaus* and the reason the area has fought off ever-encroaching chain restaurants.

These days the sheer quantity of *wirtshäuser* means that supply far outstrips demand. So when the naysayers start proclaiming that the end of the world is nigh, you could do worse than find yourself in Vienna for your last supper. — (M)

ESSAY 12
Art and soul
Shaking up schooling

___

Vienna's esteemed art school has launched a host of famous names because it so enthusiastically steeps its students in the aesthetic melting pot of the city.

by Kimberly Bradley, Monocle Vienna correspondent

Most people wouldn't even register their local art school, much less care about its legacy. But Vienna's Akademie der bildenen Künste (Academy of Fine Arts Vienna) is different. It embodies the intangibles of Viennese culture and reflects the city's idiosyncrasies. It could even be seen as a fascinating microcosm of Vienna's brilliant eccentricity and an epicentre of the cultural cross-pollination that has occurred here for centuries.

I first set foot in the academy's Semperdepot in 2013 to give a talk about art criticism. One of four academy buildings throughout the city, the Semperdepot (near Café Sperl on Gumpendorferstrasse) is a stunning triangular building

ABOUT THE WRITER: Petra Percher has called Vienna home for more than 20 years. She writes reviews for daily newspaper *Die Presse* and is the publisher of *a-list.at* where creatives reveal their favourite spots. After two decades, Augarten is still her most-cherished place in the city.

originally designed by German architect Gottfried Semper (yes, the same guy who designed the Semper Opera House in Dresden) as a storage site for the sets of Vienna's opera house and Burgtheater in the 1870s. Since 1996 it's been a buzzing art-studio building; its soaring spaces give students elbow room to experiment, create and learn. Young artists from around the world asked questions and showed me their work. I was inspired.

Later, walking through the academy's grand main building on Schillerplatz not far away, the exuberantly creative aura remained but here merged with a deeper sense of tradition and history. The headquarters of the academy since its completion in 1877, the neoclassical building has a pillared central space with a ceiling so beautiful it's hard not to gasp. The halls around it – steeped in history, quiet, naturally lit and topped with more incredible ceilings – practically embrace the student or visitor with decades of thought and creation.

Here anyone, art student or not, can dive into art in the library (which holds the university archive), the Graphics Collection, and the Pictures Gallery, the latter of which is a permanent exhibition of 180 Old Masters works. On the walls are paintings by no less than Rubens, Titian and Hieronymus Bosch; the bequeathment of the collection in 1822 created the city's very first institutional art museum.

So what does this have to do with Vienna today? The Academy was founded as a private art academy in 1688 but, like the city it sits in, it inexplicably (magically?) manages to combine the hyper traditional with the cutting-edge. Its deanery is the only one in Austria staffed entirely by women; it's also the sole Austrian university that (remarkably) refunds the national student fee. Instruction in six divisions – among them visual arts, theory, a famous restoration programme and more – follows the traditional central European form: students are admitted to the class of one "master" professor and generally stay there throughout the course of study. But professors, among them acclaimed artists such as Monica Bonvicini, Daniel Richter and favourite Austrian son Heimo Zobernig, are given free rein.

"It could even be seen as a fascinating microcosm of Vienna's brilliant eccentricity"

There's more: more than 40 per cent of the approximately 1,400 students here come from some 50 countries beyond Austria. The school bears the honour of rejecting an aspiring painter called Adolf Hitler not once but twice (he applied with undeniably terrible paintings in 1907 and 1908; the rejection crushed him) but it neither dwells upon this fact nor upon its many laurels,

Best-kept art secrets
—
01 The Academy's Graphic Collection
More than 40,000 drawings and 100,000 prints.
02 Belvedere Winterpalais
Hosts intriguing exhibitions.
03 Austrian National Library
Archive includes a million negatives.

although it certainly could. Alumni, after all, include big guns such as Egon Schiele, architects Hans Hollein and Otto Wagner, and current Austrian art star Erwin Wurm; other top names such as Friedensreich Hundertwasser and Harun Farocki have taught here.

Not long ago I visited dean Eva Blimlinger in her vast, creaky corner office in the academy's main building. Its wooden floors, tables, leather chairs and desks are piled high with books; student and alumni artworks dot the room. In her post since 2011, Blimlinger exudes the eccentric intellectualism still found in so many places in this city; it's like meeting a modern-day Gertrude Stein. She's clearly serious business but smiles warmly as she says how much she enjoys leading the school: "If it weren't fun, I wouldn't do it."

She explained the school's progressive bent: the staff and faculty male-female split is 50/50 on all levels. In 2013 the academy offered a group of refugee activists a place to convene. LGBT issues are continually addressed; artistic research incorporating other fields, such as natural science, is an increasing priority. Yet for all the topical forwardness, this school still incorporates the best of old-school. At a time in which international art education has largely gone digital (lamentably "de-skilling" young artists, according to some) the academy still offers analogue instruction, such as nude figure-drawing and workshops (metal and letterpress shops among them) that deal with art's materiality. Lots of international students come here precisely for this mix, a global art-school rarity.

Only here, I thought, as I wandered through again in early 2016, could you see a daring student exhibition on transgender issues in Xhibit, an onsite space for rotating shows, and peruse Bosch's wacky triptych *The Last Judgement* in the quiet Pictures Gallery next door (the galleries here are Vienna's best-kept secret), then have both make sense and even visually connect. Timeless tradition and truly contemporary expression coexist and co-mingle in Vienna like nowhere else. The academy is no exception. — (M)

ABOUT THE WRITER: Kimberly Bradley has worked for MONOCLE from Germany and Austria since 2009 and became Vienna correspondent in 2015.

Culture
—— In the know

Wolfgang Amadeus Mozart's heavenly music, Egon Schiele's provocative paintings and Thomas Bernhard's brilliantly acerbic prose: in all its forms, Vienna's culture is one of its greatest and longest-lasting calling cards.

The city recognises this and continually invests in its world-class museums and music halls – as well as in its upcoming geniuses – with generous grants and ongoing support. Private citizens have also helped with the funding of venues such as the MuTh theatre and the renovation of historical cinemas. It's all worth it, as the numbers show: about 900,000 people visited the Kunsthistorisches Museum alone in 2014. A new interdisciplinary biennale launched in 2015 and the Wien Museum is planning a major expansion in upcoming years.

The next few pages feature a cross-section of Vienna's top cultural offerings, from traditional to the right here, right now.

Museums
Arts and history

① Wien Museum, Innere Stadt (1st)
Warm welcome

The Wien Museum (Vienna Museum) is often overlooked by tourists and underrated by locals but it shouldn't be: it offers a fascinating overview of the city's twists, turns, glories and downfalls. The building designed by Austrian architect Oswald Haerdtl holds archaeological artefacts, exhibitions on fashion, the histories of major Vienna buildings and even the "Turkish Booty" of 1683 (the Ottomans sieged Vienna but were defeated, leaving plenty of goodies behind). There's free admission on the first Sunday of each month too.
8 Karlsplatz, 1040
+43 (0)1 505 8747
wienmuseum.at

2
Belvedere Museum,
Landstrasse (3rd)
Royal flush

The Belvedere Museum is the
closest thing Austria has to a national
collection. Located in the former
Belvedere palace complex built for
Prince Eugene of Savoy, it stretches
over several venues. The Upper
Belvedere's permanent collections
draw Klimt admirers – his famous
"The Kiss" is on display, along with
other masterpieces – and the interiors
are just as impressive as the art.

The Lower Belvedere features
a rotation of contemporary and
modern works as director Agnes
Husslein-Arco regularly mixes up
old and new in an attempt to draw
a larger audience. ("The Viennese
don't visit museums as much as they
should," he says.) Newer art can
be seen nearby at the Belvedere's
21er Haus (*see page 98*). Further
exhibitions are held in the Winter
Palace in the Innere Stadt.
6 Rennweg, 1030
+43 (0)1 7955 7134
belvedere.at

Versailles style
—
The gardens
are formal
French in
design

③
Kunsthistorisches Museum, Innere Stadt (1st)
Habsburg treasures

Along the stunning Ringstrasse, the grand boulevard that encircles the Innere Stadt, two near-identical neo-renaissance buildings face each other: one is the Natural History Museum and the other, the Kunsthistorisches Museum, is an 1891 building erected by Austro-Hungarian emperor Franz Joseph I to make the Habsburg art holdings accessible to the public.

The interior is lavish – as you enter, admire the 60-metre-high dome above the hall – and the collection is a trip through art history. Galleries feature paintings by the likes of Arcimboldo, Caravaggio, Raphael, Rubens, Vermeer and Velázquez; side wings house ancient Egyptian, Greek and Roman artefacts. As of late, the museum has been holding more modern – even contemporary – exhibitions in its upper galleries.
Maria-Theresien-Platz, 1010
+43 (0)1 525 240
khm.at

④

The Austrian Museum of Applied Arts, Innere Stadt (1st)
Shaping the future

The Austrian Museum of Applied Arts (Mak) focuses on design, architecture and contemporary and applied arts. Since taking over in 2011, director and former diplomat Christoph Thun-Hohenstein has expanded its reach with exhibitions on smart cities, communication and education. Mak spearheaded the first Vienna Biennale in 2015: *Ideas for Change* was a city-wide show considering the key question, "How do we want to live?"

Mak is packed with historical collections and has a decent experimental design space – there's even a Helmut Lang archive in the basement for style devotees. The design shop carries whimsical Austrian products you won't see in other museum shops and there's a restaurant too.
5 Stubenring, 1010
+43 (0)1 711 360
mak.at

Cultural fare

Vienna's museums offer excellent restaurants and cafés: the KHM's café is an opulent oasis under an ornate dome and in December 2015 Mak brought us a new bistro called Salon Plafond. Over at the MQ (see page 96) opt for cupcakes at Mumok or *apfelstrudel* at the Leopold Museum.

Museumsquartier
Campus of culture

Zoom, Neubau (7th)
Child's play

Zoom is an interactive children's museum with a focus on discovery. Different activities, zones and exhibitions with themes such as "Ocean" are geared towards varied age groups. Small children can make art in a studio; for those aged between eight and 14 there's an animated film-making class; and all youngsters can explore the spaces where science and art meet. Be sure to book: many activities are reservation-only. Just across the courtyard is the family-friendly Dschungel Café that is attached to children's theatre Dschungel Wien.
1 Museumsplatz, 1070
+43 (0)1 524 7908
kindermuseum.at

② Mumok, Neubau (7th)
Modern-art marvel

Mumok stands for *museum moderner kunst* (museum of modern art) and accordingly this space showcases 20th and 21st-century art with long thematic shows and temporary exhibitions.
Since German curator Karola Kraus took over in 2010 the museum has been digging into its own permanent collection that includes about 10,000 works by 1,600 artists, among them one of the most complete agglomerations of works from the Viennese Actionist movement. There is also a range of workshops, films and talks.
1 Museumsplatz, 1070
+43 (0)1 525 000
mumok.at

① Leopold Museum, Neubau (7th)
Fin-de-siècle Austria

Fans of Egon Schiele and his mentor Gustav Klimt will have a field day here. This museum is home to the private collection of one Rudolf Leopold, who, starting in the 1950s, amassed a collection of about 5,000 pieces by Austrian artists from the first half of the 20th century – before they were worth much, we might add. The Austrian government purchased his collection and built the Leopold Museum to house it in, opening in 2001.

This is the world's largest collection of Schiele's works and the curating team – which includes members of the Leopold family – expertly contextualise the pieces in exhibitions that either explore his subjects or juxtapose his work with that of other artists such as Tracey Emin. If you're hungry, the bar-café serves great Austrian food and hosts live music.
1 Museumsplatz, 1070
+43 (0)1 525 700
leopoldmuseum.org

What is the Museumsquartier?

Sometimes disparate cultural institutions combine to create a wildly successful public space. The Museumsquartier (MQ) originated in a sprawling group of buildings that were once the Habsburg empire's imperial stables. It opened in two stages starting in the late 1990s, with the final project opening in 2001.

Beyond the museums are a kids' theatre, a large Walther König art-book shop, office spaces, boutiques and several popular restaurants. In the summer, skateboarders mix with culture vultures lounging on modular outdoor furniture by PPAG architects, readers pluck books from the outdoor open libraries often parked here and diners fill up at the many outdoor restaurants.

Mixing it up
—
Old art meets new at Kunsthalle Wien

4

Kunsthalle Wien, Neubau (7th)
Experimental art

A *kunsthalle* is an exhibition hall that functions like a museum but without a permanent collection, so shows here are about the new, the risky and the experimental. In 2012 star German curator Nicolaus Schafhausen took the reins and instigated a diverse programme with exhibitions and conferences that address issues such as labour (*New Ways of Doing Nothing*, 2014) or politics (*Political Populism*, 2015). Exhibitions on Brancusi's influence or one-person shows by the likes of Isa Genzken have also been hits.

The Kunsthalle Wien's main MQ space covers several large floors but the institution also runs a project space on Karlsplatz (its original location) in a glass container surrounded by a community garden.
Kunsthalle Wien Museumsquartier
1 Museumsplatz, 1070
Kunsthalle Wien Karlsplatz
2 Treitlstrasse, 1040
+43 (0)1 521 890
kunsthallewien.at

My favourite Brancusi is 'Bird in Space'

① 21er Haus, Landstrasse (3rd)
Contemporary-art must-see

The 21er Haus is where experimental contemporary art shines under the jurisdiction of the Belvedere. But the venerable venue also has an interesting architectural history. Originally designed as the Austrian pavilion for the Brussels World Expo in 1958, the boxy glass building was moved to Vienna to act as the 20er Haus (the museum of the 20th century) in the early 1960s and soon became a hub of Austrian avant-garde art.

In early 2002 it was given to the Belvedere but the gallery didn't have funds to run it properly, so the *haus* stayed empty for years. From 2008 to 2011, Austrian architect Adolf Krischanitz revamped the building, bringing it into the 21st century and leading it to change its name. Space was added with the building of a new atrium and the return of the original 1960s porch. In terms of work on display, you'll find monographic and thematic shows, often by Austrian artists.

There's also a sculpture garden featuring works from the 1950s and 1960s, a basement art library on Austrian sculptor Fritz Wotruba, a cinema and an excellent bookshop.

1 Arsenalstrasse, 1030
+ 43 (0)1 7955 7770
21erhaus.at

I call this performance art piece 'Dog in Motion'

②
Thyssen-Bornemisza Art
Contemporary, Leopoldstadt (2nd)
Park life

The impeccably connected
Francesca von Habsburg
launched her foundation,
Thyssen-Bornemisza Art
Contemporary (TBA21), in
2002. By 2012 the ever-expanding
operation moved to Augarten park
into a spacious hall that was once
the studio of controversial sculptor
Gustinus Ambrosi.

Habsburg champions ambitious
exhibitions dealing with social and
environmental issues and featuring
big-name artists such as Olafur
Eliasson and Ernesto Neto. In
the summer, art-world thinkers
discuss ideas or perform on an
outdoor stage designed by architect
David Adjaye. For those who like
to feed their bellies as well as their
brains, café-restaurant Die Au
completes TBA21's credentials
as a happening hotspot.
1A Scherzergasse, 1020
+43 (0)1 513 985 624
tba21.org

③
Secession, Wieden (4th)
Artist-run adventure

Painter Gustav Klimt was one
of the founders of the Vienna
Secession movement; he quit the
conservative Association of Austrian
Artists to found a group that had
more artistic freedom. Since its
construction in 1898 the Secession
building has remained not only an
art-nouveau architectural wonder
– note the golden-leaf orb atop –
but also an avant-garde, artist-run
exhibition venue. "Artists deal
with art differently than museum
directors," says current president
Herwig Kempinger.

This is the place to discover the
creative stars of tomorrow: Austrians
such as post-internet sensation Oliver
Laric or international mavericks such
as British Turner Prize-winner Mark
Leckey exhibit works you won't see
anywhere else. On permanent view in
the basement is Klimt's "Beethoven
Frieze", which in itself is worth a visit.
12 Friedrichstrasse, 1010
+43 (0)1 587 5307
secession.at

①
Georg Kargl Fine Arts, Wieden (4th)
Word on the street

In 1998 dealer Georg Kargl opened
his gallery, Georg Kargl Fine Arts,
on Schleifmühlgasse, which was at
that time relatively underdeveloped.
The vast, mostly subterranean
former printing press is conducive
to both solo exhibitions and
intriguing group shows.

Kargl also operates two smaller
spaces on the same street – Box
and Permanent – the former
conceptualised by US artist Richard
Artschwager for experimental works,
the latter for long-term shows. Look
out for works by the likes of Clegg
& Guttmann and Thomas Locher.
5 Schleifmühlgasse, 1040
+43 (0)1 585 4199
georgkargl.com

②
Galerie Martin Janda, Innere
Stadt (1st)
White-cube wonder

An anchor of the Eschenbachgasse
art hub, Martin Janda's white-
cubed, concrete-floored space
never fails to deliver thought-
provoking exhibitions. Artists on
view include Swiss great Roman
Signer and US artist Joe Scanlan.
11 Eschenbachgasse, 1010
+43 (0)1 585 7371
martinjanda.at

Opened in 1923 as the Neue Galerie,
the Galerie Nächst St Stephan was
taken over by Otto Mauer in 1954.
He started showing avant garde art,
carving a space for contemporary
works in a then conservative
Vienna. Since 1978 it's been run by
art-world grande dame Rosemarie
Schwarzwälder. Now, as then, she
includes both young and old artists in
the programme. The space is a little
difficult to find, even if *nächst
St Stephan* means "next
to St Stephen's" (the cathedral).
*1 Grünangergasse, 1010
+43 (0)1 512 1266
schwarzwaelder.at*

⑥
Bäckerstrasse4, Innere Stadt (1st)
Helping hands

③
Galerie Krinzinger, Innere Stadt (1st)
Decades of artistry

Galerie Krinzinger was founded by
Tyrolean art lover Ursula Krinzinger
in 1971 and has been moving and
shaking visual-art sensibilities ever
since through its seminal shows.
Visitors can't go wrong here: the
gallery has an epic artist list, with
well-known names including Marina
Abramovic and Chris Burden.
The main gallery is an expansive
upper-storey apartment-style space
on an elegant 1st-district street, while
Krinzinger Projekte across town
shows the work of younger artists.
Always interesting.
*16 Seilerstätte, 1010
+43 (0)1 513 3006
galerie-krinzinger.at
Project space: 45 Schottenfeldgasse*

④
Galerie Emanuel Layr,
Innere Stadt (1st)
Next-generation gallery

Emanuel Layr is one of the few
youthful gallerists in the city and

shows some of Vienna's chicest
conceptual and technology-driven
artists; expect to see names such
as Julien Bismuth. But it's not all
about tech: also on the roster are
interesting eastern European
artists such as Slovakian Stano
Filko (who died in 2015) and
Bulgarian Plamen Dejanoff,
whose sculptures combine
spatial installation and craft.
*2/26 Seilerstätte, 1010
+43 (0)1 945 1791
emanuellayr.com*

In 2008 Gabriele Schober founded
this project space and platform for
artists who had recently finished their
studies as a way to help them make
the transition from art student to
working artist. With the support of
an international artist jury and local
collectors, it has worked well.
Shows here address topics such
as urbanity or "photography in the
interstices" and international guest
galleries from cities such as New
York sometimes tour exhibitions too.
Setting up a global network like this
is central to helping artists achieve
independence.
*4 Bäckerstrasse, 1010
+43 676 555 1777
baeckerstrasse4.at*

Music and theatre
The sound of Vienna

①

Burgtheater, Innere Stadt (1st)
Theatrical jewel

The Burgtheater – once the imperial theatre founded in 1741 at the bidding of Empress Maria Theresa (who wanted a stage next door), now in a grand Ringstrasse building that opened in 1888 – is one of the German-speaking world's most renowned and important stages. Over the years it has developed its own style and a "Burgtheater German" speech pattern.

Its traditional productions segued into more ground-breaking work in the 1970s and launched the careers of many directors (such as the inimitable Claus Peymann) and actors. Of the latter, English speakers might well know ensemble members Bruno Ganz (who played Adolf Hitler in *Downfall*) and Klaus Maria Brandauer (Largo, the baddie in *Never Say Never Again*). They and others perform plays written by literary greats such as Thomas Bernhard, Peter Handke and more recently Christian Kracht, mostly in German.
2 Universitätsring, 1010
+43 (0)1 514 444 140
burgtheater.at

②

Flex, Innere Stadt (1st)
Dancing on the water

Located in an old metro tunnel on the Donaukanal, this is the city's best underground venue, not only for the music – which ranges from techno to indie and rock – but also for its outstanding sound system. In summer, revellers can enjoy a beer and some fresh air on the canal too.
Abgang Augartenbrücke, 1010
+43 (0)1 533 7525
flex.at

Literaturhaus

Vienna has produced far more than its share of literary greats. Perennial hits among readers discovering the city are Thomas Bernhard – whose *Woodcutters* (1984) takes down Austrian society – and Nobel Prize-winner Elfriede Jelinek, who wrote *The Piano Teacher* (1983). New authors such as Vea Kaiser (*see page 74*) are now carrying the torch.

The Literaturhaus is a hub for this tradition, maintaining and expanding a 70,000-volume library of 20th and 21st-century Austrian literature. More than 100 free-of-charge book-related events take place here each year, many aimed at children.
literaturhaus.at

③

MuTh, Leopoldstadt (1st)
Young guns go for it

The 500-year-old Vienna Boys Choir
has a new concert hall. Situated next
to the Palais Augarten (where the
boys live, study and rehearse) at
the tip of Augarten park, it was
opened in 2012. Known as the
MuTh – it's short for Musik
und Theater – the building was
controversial: locals protested that
it was to be built on a garden site.
But since then the city has recognised
its purpose. It's a wonderful place
to hear the boys sing in the evenings
as well as at special lunchtime and
Friday afternoon concert times.
*1 Am Augartenspitz, 1020
+43 (0)1 347 8080 1020
muth.at*

④
Brut, Innere Stadt (1st)
Experimental stage

An intimate black box with 170
seats, Brut is a venue for
experimental theatre, dance and
performance. Situated in the
Künstlerhaus – the former artists'
salon dating from the late 1800s – the
site hosts about 300 productions per
season, about two thirds of them
by Austrian artists. But Brut has
plenty of international clout as well,
collaborating with small projects from
other countries. Regular workshops
in the foyer generate lively discussions
and the bar is a popular spot for
social get-togethers and musical
performances.
*5 Karlsplatz, 1010
+43 (0)1 587 8774
brut-wien.at*

⑤
Vienna State Opera, Innere
Stadt (1st)
Apex of opera

Built on the opulent Ringstrasse in
the mid-19th century and restored
after being damaged in the Second
World War, the Vienna State Opera is
one of the world's finest classical-
music venues; it opened in 1869
with a performance of Mozart's *Don
Giovanni*. Each season sees more
than 50 operatic productions staged –
perennial favourites include *Rigoletto*
– and ballet is also performed here.
Reserve well in advance; if you
decide to see a show the day it's
running you'll have to queue up a
few hours before the performance for
standing-only tickets. Luckily there
are 500 of them, and the standing-
room crowd is legendary for dishing
out loud criticism. From April to
September some performances are
live-streamed on a screen outside on
Herbert von Karajan Platz. There are
also daytime tours of the stage.
*2 Opernring, 1010
+43 (0)1 51 444
wiener-staatsoper.at*

Cinemas
Vienna's big screens

①
Metro Kinokulturhaus,
Innere Stadt (1st)
Film-lovers' cinema

After its renovation the opulent
Metro Kinokulturhaus, part of the
Filmarchiv Austria, reopened in 2015.
Now cinephiles have two screening
rooms and three exhibition halls to
enjoy. The venue also hosts two art
shows each year.

The cinema's wood-panelled,
red-velvet grandeur was retained:
the building was constructed in
1893 and converted into a theatre
in 1924. Thanks to architect Gregor
Eichinger's efforts, viewers can now
look into the screening space from
the foyer through a glass wall.
4 Johannesgasse, 1010
+43 (0)1 512 1803
filmarchiv.at

I've got
the best
perch
in the
house!

Keeping it real

Since 1999, Vienna has
financially supported its
programmkinos (arthouse
cinemas) through the Vienna
film fund. Cinemas such as
Admiral, Burgkino and even
Gartenbau benefit from the
programme and thus avoid
being dependent on a diet of
blockbuster films.

The city on screen

Vienna occupies a special place in cinema, through its memorable onscreen portrayals from *The Third Man* in 1949 to *Before Sunrise* 46 years later. A dedicated agency now exists to support and promote the city's enduring star power. Established in 2009, the Vienna Film Commission is focused on creating an environment that's friendlier than ever for film-makers. It supports film, TV, documentary, student, and commercial production companies keen on shooting in the historic hub of Europe.

Besides scouting locations, easing the process of applying for permits and helping organise on-location shoots, the Vienna Film Commission assists production companies with funding initiatives such as Film Location Austria and the Vienna Film Fund, designed to strengthen the city's role in the industry and back productions with substantial grants.

One of the first movies that CEO Marijana Stoisits and her team helped bring to fruition was David Cronenberg's *A Dangerous Method*. Their latest – but by no means last – success is a biggie: *Mission: Impossible – Rogue Nation*.

② Votivkino, Alsergrund (9th)
Small package, good things

This lovely cinema passed the century mark in 2012. It never fails to provide a thought-provoking programme with films shown in their original language (German-speaking countries tend to dub, so this is a special treat). Small, intimate and with an arthouse flavour.
Währingerstrasse 12, 1090
+43 (0)1 317 3571
votivkino.at

③ Austrian Film Museum, Innere Stadt (1st)
Reel deal

Situated inside the Albertina art museum – itself housed in an opulent Habsburg palace – the Austrian Film Museum has overseen the preservation and restoration of films, including delicate nitrate film and artefacts (31,000 of them dating to the late 1800s), since the 1960s. These prints aren't just hidden away in the vaults: a lively programme – recently including screenings of films by John Cassavetes, Chantal Akerman and even the Marx Brothers – is always on tap for visitors to enjoy.
1 Augustinerstrasse, 1010
+43 (0)1 533 7054
filmmuseum.at

④ Gartenbaukino, Innere Stadt (1st)
Prime candidate

Dating to 1919 and rebuilt in the early 1960s, this cinema – situated in between the Palais Coburg and the Stadtpark – is the primary screening venue for the annual Viennale film festival. And with good reason: the main theatre holds 736 people and the 1960s architecture is still intact.

The festival almost didn't happen when the cinema went bankrupt in 2002. But the operation was saved by private supporters and the city of Vienna, since it was the last centrally located "premiere cinema". These days the venue hosts events, musical performances and exhibitions.
12 Parkring, 1010
+43 (0)1 512 2354
gartenbaukino.at

Vienna on film

01 The Joyless Street, 1925: Although filmed in a Berlin film studio, this silent drama offers a vivid and expressionistic account of poverty among a group of unfortunates in the Austrian capital.

02 The Third Man, 1949: A crime thriller set in an unadorned postwar Vienna; fans can take a ride, as star Orson Welles does, on the Ferris wheel at the Prater.

03 Before Sunrise, 1995: Celine (Julie Delpy) and Jesse (Ethan Hawke) interrupt their train journey and spend a night getting to know each other in the city.

04 The Piano Teacher, 2001: Erika (Isabelle Huppert), a piano instructor and failed concert pianist, begins an affair with a younger student. Vienna's musical legacies take centre stage.

05 Museum Hours, 2012: Jem Cohen paints a portrait of gentle companionship and Vienna's unobserved fringes in this film.

06 Woman in Gold, 2015: Vienna's artistic legacy plays a major role in this film about a Jewish woman who takes on the government to recover a lost painting by Gustav Klimt.

Media
In print and on air

Radio
On the waves

In Vienna airwaves are full of surprises: English commentary; tunes sung in dialect; and even a classical-music station, Radio Stephansdom, run by the archdiocese. Generally Viennese radio breaks down in to public (Austrian broadcaster ORF radio reaches 62.8 per cent of Austrians each day) and commercial (stations such as Superfly, which plays funk and soul, or the self-explanatory LoungeFM).

Especially loved is FM4, a branch of ORF that broadcasts live sessions, multilingual talk radio and music that refreshingly skews local. Founded in the mid-1990s, what began as an evening programme became its own 24-hour frequency. Programming is more than 50 per cent in English and DJs such as Natalie Brunner and Alexander Hertl assemble their own playlists. "It's about maintaining trust," says producer and co-founder Martin Pieper. "We have to keep our authenticity."
fm4.orf.at

①
Media
Reading material

Who says print is dead? In Austria it's alive and well. For those who don't read German there's ❶ *Metropole*, an expat magazine covering events and issues in Vienna in English. Austria's weekly news magazine is ❷ *Profil*, which touches on longer-form commentary. Then comes a selection of fun indies such as ❸ *Spike*, a smarty-pants art magazine partially in English, and ❹ *Biber*, a pointed but often very clever magazine that covers issues surrounding immigration. Much of it is written by first and second-generation Austrians with immigrant backgrounds. ❺ *Falter* – a shining example of how an opinionated independent weekly can survive – often breaks political and cultural stories. And finally you have ❻ *Der Standard* and ❼ *Die Presse*, both well-produced daily newspapers with supplementary Sunday sections and commentary. The former is centrist-libertarian, the latter a few steps to the left.

❷
Newsstands, citywide
Print on demand

One of the strangest sights in Vienna – and there's surprisingly strong competition – are daily newspapers hanging from plastic contraptions outdoors. Buyers are meant to throw a coin into a slot when they take one and remarkably this honesty system works. Local papers and magazines are also available in any tobacco store – look for the "Tabak Trafik" sign – but dedicated international and magazine shops are harder to find.

Thalia, a noted bookshop chain from Germany, is as good as it gets when it comes to the international and local press, with five locations in the city. Walther König has a wonderful arts and design-based magazine and press section in its bookshop in the Museumsquartier, while Zamm Coffee and Books is a lovely café where magazines and books – including MONOCLE's titles – are available to buy and read.
thalia.at;
zammcoffee.at

I'm a fan of the Superfly station

Design and architecture
—— Anything and everything

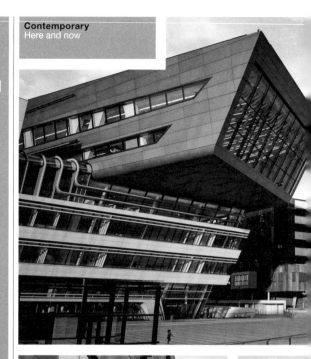

Contemporary
Here and now

Vienna's reputation rests largely on its fin de siècle golden age when the likes of artist Gustav Klimt, architect Otto Wagner and psychoanalyst Sigmund Freud made the city a centre of European culture. Now, after decades of insularity, Vienna is once again emerging as an important hub for architecture, art and design – thanks in part to affordable rents, inner-city manufacturing credentials and exciting new initiatives by both homegrown and international creatives.

Lovers of architecture have long made the Austrian capital a place of pilgrimage: its built environment incorporates the key genres and forms known since the Middle Ages. Gothic churches sit beside Baroque and imperial dwellings, there are landmark buildings commissioned between 1918 and 1934 (the Red Vienna period) and majestic Jugendstil (Viennese art nouveau) edifices stand alongside contemporary creations. Here are some of our favourite spots.

Shape shifters
——
The campus is a mixture of angles and curves

① University of Economics and Business in Vienna campus, Leopoldstadt (2nd)
Bright future

Vienna's Wirtschaftsuniversität Wien (WU) calls itself a "university of the future", and its new campus in the city's 2nd district would certainly look at home in a science-fiction film. Opened in 2013, it features a collection of colourful and eye-catching buildings that have been designed by some of the world's most renowned contemporary architects, such as Zaha Hadid – who designed the Library and Learning Centre – and Sir Peter Cook.

"This university is about being here," says Jean Pierre Bolívar of Austrian firm BUSarchitektur, which developed the masterplan and designed some of the buildings. The campus is located in a former red-light district not far from the popular Prater amusement park.
1 Welthandelsplatz, 1020
wu.ac.at

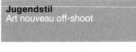

DC Tower 1, Donaustadt (22nd)
Height of hi-tech

Built on former swampland on the northern bank of the Danube, the 250-metre DC Tower 1 is Austria's tallest building. The site was originally meant to host a World Expo but the plans were scrapped following a referendum. Instead it became home to the sprawling Donau City, Vienna's take on a cutting-edge business centre.

According to its architect Dominique Perrault, the tower, with its memorable wave-like façade, should become a "new gateway" into the city. The landmark will soon be joined by a second, smaller tower.
*7 Donau-City-Strasse, 1220
viennadc.at*

(3)

Haas-Haus, Innere Stadt (1st)
Controversial creation

The glass-and-stone Haas-Haus is often described as one of Vienna's uglier buildings. Built in 1990 by

Hans Hollein, it is the third building to bear the name of carpet-maker Philipp Haas: the first was burnt to the ground in 1945, the second torn down in 1986 after angry protests.

This third building is no less contradictory. One of the last big projects completed in the Innere Stadt before it gained Unesco World Heritage status, it caused a reaction that Adolf Loos would have been all too familiar with (*see page 111*). Today the building is home to a hotel, shops and a restaurant.
Stephansplatz, 1010

The Haas-Haus looks better upside down

Take note
——
The façade is made up of marble plates

①

Österreichische Postsparkasse (1st)
Cashing in

A pioneering creation of Otto Wagner, the Österreichische Postsparkasse (Postal Savings Bank) is sometimes cited as the most significant work by the father of modern architecture and one of the city's best examples of the second phase of Jugendstil (art nouveau). It was built between 1904 and 1912 on the eastern sweep of Vienna's Ringstrasse and is particularly recognised for its functional spatial solution, industrial motifs and the glass roof of its central hall. Wagner employed the most modern materials of the period in his use of aluminium and glass blocks alongside marble slabs secured with bolts.

Wagner pushed the limits of the architect's profession by designing not only the structure but also the entire interior including the furniture, much of which is in use today. The bank now doubles as a museum and is well worth a visit.
2 Georg-Coch-Platz, 1010
ottowagner.com

Box clever
—
Formal gardens echo the building's lines

Wienzeile ensemble, Mariahilf (6th)
It takes two

These two apartment blocks overlooking the Naschmarkt were built between 1898 and 1899 by Otto Wagner and are famous for their decorative façades and iron balconies. The Majolikahaus at number 40 represents the floral strain of Jugendstil, with its jumble of roses and plants, while the white and gold of the adjacent house at number 38 echoes the nearby Secession building (*see page 99*). Also of note are its rounded corner and protruding iron-and-glass porch. Wagner acted as the contractor for this project and paid for the weather-proof tiles of the Majolikahaus himself.
38 and 40 Linke Wienzeile, 1060

Vienna Workshops

Wiener Werkstätte (Vienna Workshops) was a co-operative enterprise founded in 1903 by artist Koloman Moser and architect-designer Josef Hoffmann. Inspired by the UK's arts-and-crafts movement, it aimed to restore artisanal values to the increasingly industrialised Austrian society.

The enterprise had close ties to the Vienna Secession (*see page 99*) led by Gustav Klimt and spanned everything from jewellery to fashion and furniture, bringing all aspects of life into a *gesamtkunstwerk* (total work of art). The movement became known for its elegant and innovative "square style", which influenced Bauhaus in Germany as well as the work of US architect Frank Lloyd Wright.

②
Purkersdorf Sanatorium, Purkersdorf
Thinking straight

Considered among the most important of Vienna's modern-era buildings, this sanatorium was completed in 1905 by Josef Hoffmann, celebrated architect-designer and co-founder of both the Vienna Secession (*see page 99*) and Vienna Workshops (*see right*).

The building's plain façade (it's reduced to lines, squares and rectangles) and exquisite interiors render it one of the finest specimens of the cubic-geometric phase of Jugendstil (Viennese art nouveau). It once housed nervous-ailment specialists, who treated luminaries such as composer Gustav Mahler.
60-70 Wiener Strasse, 3002

I've always wanted to live in a palace. Where's the Schönbrunn?

④ Looshaus, Innere Stadt (1st)
Plain statement

Located in the heart of the Innere
Stadt at the head of a fashionable
shopping street and in plain view of
the Hofburg, this is perhaps the most
well-known – and controversial –
building of groundbreaking architect
Adolf Loos. Completed in 1912, its
façade was so defiantly void of
decoration that Emperor Franz
Joseph I couldn't bear to look at it.

The ground floor and mezzanine
were occupied by gentlemen's
outfitters Goldmann & Salatsch,
while the upper floors were
apartments. Today it houses a branch
of Raiffeisenbank – nip in for a peek
at the interiors, including the
staircase's marble-and-glass finish.
3 Michaelerplatz, 1010

Middle Ages and Baroque
Blasts from the past

① St Stephen's Cathedral, Innere
Stadt (1st)
Symbol of the city

St Stephen's Cathedral, with its
colourful zigzag-patterned roof
of 230,000 glazed tiles and its
136-metre-high steeple, marks the
centre of the 1st district. A gem of
medieval gothic architecture, the
14th-century cathedral, affectionately
known as *Steffl*, has played a key role
in Austrian history.

Along with the giant Ferris wheel
in the Prater amusement park, St
Stephen's has become the de facto
symbol of Vienna and appeared
extensively in art, literature and
cinema. It is the tallest structure
in the Innere Stadt.
3 Stephansplatz, 1010
stephanskirche.at

② Schönbrunn Palace, Hietzing (13th)
Storied grandeur

Built in the late 17th century by
Johann Bernhard Fischer von Erlach,
the man who shaped the tastes of the

Habsburg empire, this richly
decorated rococo-style 1,441-room
palace was once a summer residence
for royalty.

The palace and its grounds (which
house the oldest zoo in the world)
were made a Unesco World Heritage
site in 1996. Schönbrunn has
witnessed its fair share of history,
from the death of Emperor Franz
Joseph I to the 1961 meeting between
US president John F Kennedy and
Soviet premier Nikita Khrushchev.
47 Schönbrunner Schlosstrasse, 1130
schoenbrunn.at

③
University of Vienna,
Innere Stadt (1st)
Artsy school

The University of Vienna is one of
the oldest in Europe – it celebrated
its 650th anniversary in 2015 – but
its main building on Ringstrasse
is far younger, dating from the
mid-1880s. It was designed by
Austrian architect and professor
Heinrich von Ferstel, who helped
shape the entire 19th-century
Ringstrasse ensemble.

Reminiscent of an Italian
palazzo, the university has a
spacious inner yard encircled by
busts of its most famous alumni,
including Sigmund Freud, Ludwig
Wittgenstein and Erwin
Schrödinger. The artist Gustav
Klimt painted the murals for the
ceiling of the Main Ceremonial
Chamber but they were sadly
destroyed by retreating German
troops in the Second World War.
The grand library and reading
room remain.
1 Universitätsring, 1010
univie.ac.at

Off the shelf
——
The library at
the university
is Austria's
largest

④
Austrian Parliament Building,
Innere Stadt (1st)
Pillars of society

Built by Theophil von Hansen,
one of Vienna's most prolific
architects of the late-19th century,
the parliament building is a
characteristic example of the then
popular historicist style, which
harked back to Greek and Roman
traditions. Accordingly, the place
appears to be nothing so much as
an antique temple, complete with
an elaborate frontispiece and dozens
of statues, the whole dominated by
a figure of Greek goddess Athena in
front of the entrance.

The building sustained heavy
damage during the Second World
War and large parts of its grand
interiors were completely destroyed.
Fortunately, Von Hansen's vision
was lovingly restored in the years
that followed the war, during the
national resurgence that led to the
formation of the new Austrian
republic in 1955.
3 Doktor-Karl-Renner-Ring, 1017
parlament.gv.at

⑤
Hofburg Palace, Innere Stadt (1st)
Historical hub

With its earliest wings dating from
the 13th century, the Hofburg Palace
is steeped in Austria's story: this is
where Emperor Joseph II came up
with his reforms in the 1780s, where
the delegates of the 1815 Congress
of Vienna danced and where the
penultimate emperor, Franz Joseph I,
held his audiences.

The palace now houses the
offices of the president, the HQ
of the Organisation for Security
and Co-operation in Europe and
the Austrian National Library, all
encased in the richly decorated stone
of the Middle Ages and the gold
of the Baroque.
Michaelerkuppel, 1010
hofburg-wien.at

Architecture explorations

Die Österreichische Gesellschaft
für Architektur, founded
in 1965, is the country's
oldest architectural body.
It runs discussions and the
Architekturtage national festival,
plus guided tours of listed
buildings and construction sites.
oegfa.at

6

Rathaus, Innere Stadt (1st)
Better together

The airy Rathaus (city hall) was completed in 1883 to replace the cramped old building and give pride of place to the newly laid Ringstrasse boulevard. With elements of gothic and Baroque style, it opens onto a large square that serves as a staging ground for public events from rock concerts to markets – this is where you'll find Vienna's biggest Christmas market, for example.

Its central 105-metre-tall tower echoes the steeples of the nearby neo-gothic Votive Church, built a few years before to mark the attempted assassination of Emperor Franz Joseph I on the same spot.
1 Friedrich-Schmidt-Platz, 1010
wien.gv.at

Red Vienna
Socialist structures

KARL MARX-HOF

(1)

Karl Marx Hof, Döbling (19th)
Superblock citadel

Vienna's local government is Europe's largest landlord, owning almost 25 per cent of properties in the city. Many of them sprouted between 1918 and 1934 during a period of socialist government known as Red Vienna, which made a massive social-housing push in response to a shortage of affordable homes. Several superblocks were erected and the largest of them all is Karl-Marx-Hof.

A veritable fortress of socialist solidarity, it is 1km long with about 1,400 apartments and has been stormed by both fascist paramilitaries and Soviet troops during Austria's turbulent past. Its proud and powerful exterior is in contrast to its homely garden courtyards and a stately *cour d'honneur*. It also houses a museum dedicated to the Red Vienna period; check for opening times before heading here.
Halteraugasse 7, 1190
dasrotewien-waschsalon.at

Island life

Engineers had long been looking for a way to protect Vienna from the flood-prone Danube, work that culminated in the 1980s with the cutting of a deep new channel. The dredged land was used to create the Donauinsel (Danube Island), today one of the city's best-loved leisure areas.

I've packed supplies so I can maximise my architecture explorations

Housing complexes

With the birth of the Second Republic following the Second World War – the first was formed after the dissolution of the Habsburg monarchy in 1918 – and the gradual growth in prosperity and population that it brought, Vienna faced another housing problem. The solution was in the construction of huge complexes such as Am Schöpfwerk (1981) and Alt Erlaa (1985) on the southern outskirts.

Gasometer is a more recent development. It consists of four red-brick gas tanks converted into a residential-and-shopping estate by a team including Jean Nouvel and Coop Himmelblau.

Freshen up
—
The pool reopened after refurbishment in 2012

2
Amalienbad, Favoriten (10th)
Bigger splash

This impressive swimming pool can accommodate up to 1,300 people and is one of Vienna's largest. It's also an architectural landmark, with elements of Red Vienna roughness, a few flourishes of Jugendstil decadence and a layout that harks back to Roman baths. It is named after Amalie Polzer, one of Austria's first female politicians, and was damaged during the Second World War; since then its magnificent glass roof has not opened.

There's a nude sauna but consult the timetable before barging in: there are specific times allocated for mixed, male and female bathing.
Reumannplatz 23, 1100
wien.gv.at

③
Reumannhof, Margareten (5th)
Palace for the people

This superblock is named after
Jakob Reumann, Vienna's first
socialist mayor. Here, more than
in any other Red Vienna housing
complex, you'll find references
to that other important layer of
Vienna's architectural history: the
Baroque. The central block is flanked
by wings and its layout alludes to
the nearby Schönbrunn Palace;
little wonder critics ironically named
such structures *volkswohnungspaläste*
(people's apartment-palaces).
Smaller than the Karl Marx Hof,
the building was nevertheless
designed to be self-sufficient
with shops, art studios, a central
laundry and kindergarten.
100-110 Margaretengürtel, 1050

Brutalism
Raw looks

①

Living Tomorrow complex,
Rudolfsheim-Fünfhaus (15th)
Block parity

Built in 1979 as part of a
design competition, this vast
housing complex by Wilhelm
Holzbauer resembles a sturdy
ship steaming its passengers
towards a bright future. It also
aims at being an autonomous
building, with terraces, gardens
and services. Although its 292
apartments are all different
in size and layout, its exterior
is flawlessly symmetrical.
6-10 Weiglgasse, 1150

②
Wotruba church, Liesing (23rd)
Concrete belief

The Church of the Holy Trinity,
popularly known as the Wotruba
church, looks more like an ecstatic
pile of blocks than a building. And
no wonder: its creator is sculptor
Fritz Wotruba, renowned for his
spare, abstract images of the
human form.

This two-storey structure is
made entirely out of reinforced
concrete. There are 152 different
pieces of it bolted together to frame
plate-glass windows offering views
from its hillside location in an
outlying area close to the Vienna
Woods. It has a strong sculptural
quality but Wotruba was actually
inspired by, if not a direct imitation
of, the gothic Chartres Cathedral in
France; he said he wanted to "form
something that shows that poverty
needn't mean ugliness, that
renunciation can occur within
surroundings which are beautiful
though extremely simple".
*1 Ottillingerplatz 1, 1230
georgenberg.at*

Mid-century design

Austrian architecture has
mostly flourished but its
development stalled in the
mid-20th century amid the
rise of Nazism. Even so the
anschluss – the union of
Hitler's Germany and Austria
– left an architectural legacy,
most notably the six
anti-aircraft towers (*flaktürme*)
erected in the last years of
the Second World War. They
encircle the city centre and are
almost impossible to tear down
due to their solid construction.

The desire to move on from
wartime hardships led to the
emergence of pioneering new
projects. One such is the
Strandbad Gänsehäufel, a
recreation area at the Alte
Donau, a rerouted lake-like
arm of the Danube created
by the river's flood-regulation
measures in the late 1870s.

Another 1950s build is the
Ringturm, presiding over the
northwestern curve of the
Ringstrasse. A lighthouse atop
the structure forecasts the
weather using colour, while the
entrance hall hosts exhibitions
about Austrian architecture.

3
Vienna International Center,
Donaustadt (22nd)
International rescue

Visitors to Vienna will find that the
"Blue Danube" made famous by
Johann Strauss II is not actually
blue but at one time they may not
have spotted it at all. The great river,
sliced in half by an artificial island,
flows through a distant suburb of
the city that has only been developed
in the past few decades. Change
was kickstarted in 1979 by the
construction of this brutalist Y-shaped
complex known as UNO City. It offers
daily guided tours giving an insight
into its work and, as one of the UN's
four headquarters, cements Vienna's
historic stature as a seat of power.
5 Wagramer Strasse, 1220
unvienna.org

Guiding light
———
Austrian architects can have it
tough in the face of regulation.
Among the organisations
lending a helping hand is IG
Architektur, based near the
Haus des Meeres. It runs
members' training and hosts
public discussions on urban
planning and sustainability.
ig-architektur.at

Eclecticism
Viennese whirl

①
Central Savings Bank,
Favoriten (10th)
Building of note

One of the first major buildings
by Günther Domenig, the most
prominent architect of the Graz
school, this building is expressive
and functional in equal measure: it
combines a decidedly biomorphic
aesthetic (its dramatic stainless-
steel façade looks like something
full of bones, tendons and joints)
with modern technology. It
prompted heated debate when it
opened in 1979 but has since
become a staple of Austrian
architecture and was listed in 2005.
It no longer functions as a bank;
today it's home to a café, retail
space and offices.
Favoritenstrasse 118, 1100

That's my 10th cathedral snapped today

②
VHS Wiener Urania, Innere Stadt (1st)
Intellectual space

Named after the muse of
astronomy, this observatory was
completed in 1910 by Max Fabiani,
a student of Otto Wagner. Today
the building hosts the Viennale film
festival and various lectures; Thomas
Mann, Hermann Hesse and Arthur
Schnitzler have all read here.
1 Uraniastrasse, 1010
+43 (0)1 891 74 101 000
planetarium-wien.at

①
Karlsplatz Stadtbahn Station,
Innere Stadt (1st)
Art deco lines

Along with several other stations
on Vienna's original railway line,
this spot is noted for its exquisite
Jugendstil beauty. All were
designed by Otto Wagner, who
dreamed of an "expanding city"
of which the Stadtbahn, or city
railway, was a key element.
His 1893 general plan for Vienna
was never executed but he lent
tremendous impetus to the
development of the city as a
modern metropolis.

The two steel-and-marble
Karlsplatz pavilions were taken
down during the construction
of the U-Bahn in the late 1970s
and later re-erected to become
the Wien Museum and a café.
Karlsplatz, 1010
wienmuseum.at

③
Hundertwasserhaus,
Landstrasse (3rd)
Plan it organic

Avante-garde artist and architect
Friedensreich Hundertwasser,
whose self-selected middle names
were Regentag (rainy day) and
Dunkelbunt (darkly multi-
coloured), left an indelible mark on
Vienna's cityscape. A campaigner
for natural, organic forms, he
abhorred straight lines, calling
them "the rotten foundation of
our doomed civilisation". Instead,
in both his artwork and buildings,
he cultivated asymmetry, bright,
contrasting colours and natural
vegetation – most famously in his
fairytale-like Hundertwasserhaus,
a block of council flats in Vienna
that opened in 1986.

The building has more than
200 trees and shrubs on the roof
and balconies. The architect's other
notable works in the city include the
Kunst Haus Wien museum and the
district heating plant in Spittelau.
13 Untere Weissgerberstrasse, 1030
kunsthauswien.com

②
Wien Hauptbahnhof, Favoriten
(10th)
Making tracks

Completed in 2014, the
Hauptbahnhof is Austria's most
important rail terminus, with the
capacity to handle 1,100 trains
a day. It's also an architectural
marvel, formed of 14 76-metre-long
steel diamonds, each with a 180 sq m
window set in its centre. Architect
Albert Wimmer describes it as an
"homage to a sheet of music",
symbolising Vienna's rich musical
history. It also highlights that
peculiarly Viennese mix of past and
future: on one side sits the Belvedere
palace complex, on the other a
sparkling new urban development.
107 Alfred-Adler-Strasse, 1100
oebb.at

(3)

Wien Mitte station,
Landstrasse (3rd)
Gateway to Vienna

Since late 2012 Wien Mitte
station's shiny terminal has served
as the first point of call for many
arrivals to the city: 250,000 people
pass through every day. This
three-storey building, which
includes a shopping mall and office
space, was 20 years in the making
thanks to complex land-use issues
and a series of ditched architecture
bids. A public-private partnership
got things running in 2006 with
contributions from the German
architecture bureau Ortner &
Ortner, the firm responsible for a
large part of the Museumsquartier.
1c Landstrasser Hauptstrasse, 1030
wienmitte-themall.at

Visual identity
Capital letters

Durchgänge, citywide
Short cuts

Vienna is easy to navigate but if
you need to cut corners many
buildings in the Innere Stadt and
other districts have *durchgänge* or
pawlatschen – passageways that
slice through blocks and blocks of
flats. Some of these are now
bustling shopping arcades but
others remain calm, peaceful places
where neighbours can chat in the
evening over coffee and hang out
their laundry to dry.
  There are more than 20 of
these thoroughfares located in the
durchhäuser (through-houses),
mostly built around the mid-19th
century to connect two parallel
busy streets. Many inner yards
are also open to visitors.

②
Names of buildings, citywide
Formal address

Go down any Viennese street and you will notice that houses often have names. In the case of, say, the Karl Marx Hof there is no confusion as to who is being honoured but other buildings, especially those from before the collapse of the Austro-Hungarian Empire in 1918, will likely refer to an original owner or architect or their business or place of origin. Others are named after saints (Saint George is a particular favourite), horses or trivia.

It is rare to hear people in Vienna actually use these often cumbersome names but they reflect a sense of the continuity that pervades the city.

③
Colour palette, citywide
Shades of the city

In the Innere Stadt and other central districts the dominant shades are either sparkling white with a few gold trimmings or beige and warm earth tones, leading celebrated Russian author Anton Chekhov to compare Viennese buildings to "biscuits for tea".

The further away from the city centre, however, the greyer and more subdued the street palette becomes. This is a reflection not only of the rougher nature of the outer districts but also of the materials used in their construction: large parts of the double-digit districts were built in the 1960s and 1970s using prefabricated panels.

④
Double-glazed windows, citywide
Clearly Viennese

The double-glazed window first appeared in Viennese architecture at the turn of the 19th century and became a regular feature during the Gründerzeit (from around the late 1840s to the late 1870s), when Vienna enjoyed an economic and demographic boom that brought it truly international stature.

Often accompanied by decorative framing and columns, these windows survived into following periods and appear in some new builds too. Known as *wiener kastenfenster* (Viennese box windows), they feature highly characteristic handles and opening mechanisms and are typically finished in white or brown.

Future developments
———
Vienna's population will reach two million by 2029 so construction is rife. The Sonnwendviertel development will add about 5,000 flats, while on the site of the city's first airfield a whole district, Seestadt Aspern, is being built from scratch.

These 'biscuit buildings' are making me hungry

Sport and fitness
—— Activities for all seasons

The best options for keeping fit on your stay in the Austrian capital make the most of its natural assets. Why not mix up your normal routine with a few stolen hours on the slopes, a cycle along the Danube, a hike to the Stefaniewarte watch tower or a jog through the Prater? Alte Donau neighbourhood is also a popular recreational spot, offering swimming, sailing and kayaking.

So read on for our round-up of the best ways to work out while breathing in the open air and soaking up the city's sights. And for those days when the weather's poor? Head to Therme Wien or the grand Amalienbad baths, or book an appointment at one of our favourite grooming spots for some pampering and relaxation.

Wiener Eistraum, Innere Stadt (1st)
Winter wonderland

From mid-January till March, the square in front of city hall is transformed into an ice rink that whirls day and night with skaters to the strains of waltz. Once the sun goes down the grand building is lit up, adding to the romance and whimsy.

Those who prefer to stay off the ice can watch the afternoon curling practice sessions or drink hot aromatic punch and sample traditional food from the stands.
+ 43 (0)1 409 0040
wienereistraum.com

Those toddies of glühwein punch might have been a bad idea

Skiing, Stuhleck
Where the Viennese go to ski

Most snow fanatics associate Austrian ski holidays with lands further west but less than one hour's drive from Vienna is Stuhleck, one of the country's first ski areas. Its 24km of groomed runs, six-person chairlifts, fun parks for snowboarders and mountain restaurants sit on the highest peak in the Eastern Alps. There's plenty of variety here for daytrippers, weekend warriors, and ski bums coming from Vienna. Ski in the week and you might have the slopes largely to yourself. Bliss.
6c Bundesstrasse, 8684,
Spital am Semmering
Snow line: + 43 385 3333
Lift info: + 43 385 3270
stuhleck.at

How to get there
——
Stuhleck is an easy drive from the city down the S6 freeway but those without their own wheels can still hit the slopes. Trains run regularly from Wien Hauptbahnhof to Semmering, where you can jump on a bus to the resort, and various coach companies offer transport and ski pass combos.

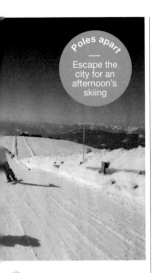

Poles apart
———
Escape the city for an afternoon's skiing

Ⓢ
Cross-country skiing
Powder runs

When temperatures hit freezing in Vienna there may very well be snow. With the mercury below minus 2C the Jesuitenwiese meadow on the Prater is transformed into a toboggan run and as soon as the snow is deeper than 20cm, the Snow Sports Academy prepares eight different trails in the city for cross-country skiing. In the second district an 8km skiing route stretches to central Praterstern; on the Donauinsel a 12km trail leads from the Reichsbrücke to the Steinspornbrücke; and to the southwest you can circle the Pappelteich.
wien.gv.at/freizeit/sportamt/ arten/winter

Grooming

01 **Brothers barbershop, Neubau:** This relative newcomer to the scene was opened by brothers Ilya Sovtsov and Ivan Perevarin in the city's creative Neubau district in 2015. They enlisted the steady hands of barber Patrick Ridlmaier who leads the team in haircuts, hot-towel shaves and beard trims, while customers recline in retro-style barber chairs and leather couches.
babershop.wien

02 **Salon Er-Ich, Innere Stadt:** With nearly 20 years' experience cutting and styling hair in Vienna, Erich Joham is an established name in the business. His eponymous studio sits off the bustling Schwedenplatz square. Inside it has the feel of a cosy 18th-century Viennese salon.
+43 (0)1 535 6677

03 **Sacher spa, Innere Stadt:** For some Viennese indulgence, head to the fifth floor of Hotel Sacher Wien (see page 27) and book a massage at Sacher Spa. A house speciality is the cacao-butter massage and mask.
sacher.com

(see page 27)

Weatherproof
Indoor exercise

Amalienbad baths, Favoriten (10th)
Make a splash

Having already graced these pages for its impressive Red Vienna architecture (see page 115), this decadent indoor pool is one of our favourite options to chase the black line in scenic surrounds. The indoor complex keeps temperatures warm and beside the 33-metre-long main pool, there's also a small children's pool and a training pool. There are saunas too.
23 Reumannplatz, 1100
+43 (0)1 607 4747
wien.gv.at

(see page 115)

John Harris Fitness, Innere Stadt (1st)
Heavy duty

Vienna prides itself on its outdoor assets, which may explain why the choice of gyms is uninspiring. But if you find yourself hankering for a treadmill or a set of dumbbells, the John Harris outpost in Schillerplatz is a good – and always spotlessly clean – option. Day passes are €38.
5 Nibelungengasse, 1010
+43 (0)1 587 3710
johnharris.at

Therme Wien, Favoriten (10th)
Steam cleaning

Austria's largest thermal baths has 26 pools, 24 saunas and steam rooms, 2,500 loungers and a 6,000 sq m health and fitness area. The thermal spa is a stream running through the grounds that consists of a series of waterfalls and fountains. Follow the stream to end up at an indoor pool that flows into the outdoor area; the heated loungers are a special treat. The spa also boasts an aroma room with waterbeds, grotto, fire lounge, cinema and "thermal library" where visitors can dive into an audiobook as they relax.
14 Kurbadstrasse, 1100
+43 (0)1 680 09
thermewien.at

❶

Hiking, Döbling
Into the hills

Venture out of the Innere Stadt when the sun's out and you'll see people striding toward the hills. Vienna's Forestry Office has mapped more than 500km of trails including 11 city hiking paths, all of which are easily accessed by public transport.

For the best view of the city, catch the D line tram out to Nussdorf and follow the signs for the City Hiking Trail 1. This jaunt into the Vienna Woods is a steady climb past vineyards and up to Stefaniewarte, which at 484 metres high affords unspoiled views back to the city. The viewing tower was designed by Ferdinand Fellner and Hermann Helmer and opened in 1887 for the Belgian royal Crown Princess Stefanie – after whom it's named. The hike is a 11km round trip.
kahlenberg-wien.at

Three more hikes

01 Jubiläumswarte, Penzing: Explore the wild side of the city on this trek through Dehnepark, a lovely forest and nature park to the west of the city centre. Catch the 49 tram to Linzer Strasse, then follow the trail north through the park, stopping after 7km at the Jubiläumswarte observation tower for great views of the city (if you've still energy left for the stairs up).
wien.gv.at/english/leisure/hiking/path4.html

02 Bisamberg, Korneuburg: Starting at Josef-Flandorfer-Strasse (get there on tram 31) go northeast into the large park surrounding Bisamberg hill. There's plenty of space for kids to run around on this 10km trek through some of Vienna's finest greenery, and en route there's the *heurigen* Magdalenenhof for a hearty energy boost.
wien.gv.at/english/leisure/hiking/path5.html

03 Laaer Berg, Favoriten: This 15km walk takes you through the landscape and parks around the foot of the Laaer Berg hill to the southern outskirts of Vienna. Take tram 67 to Altes Landgut and follow the route either east or west – it forms a loop that will take you back where you started, passing parks, lakes and the homely Brückenwirt restaurant.
wien.gv.at/english/leisure/hiking/path7.html

Let's head up to the tower for a bird's-eye-view

Still waters
——
Sail away at the Alte Donau

②
Swimming at Alte Donau,
Donaustadt (22nd)
Urban swimming oasis

Conjure up a vision of a central
European river paradise, with water
clean enough to drink, banks lined
with old-growth trees and swans
gliding through rustling reeds.
Amazingly you can find this just
seven subway stops from Vienna's
city centre: as the Alte Danube
(Old Danube – a former arm of
the great river, now more like a lake)
gently curves around Donaustadt's
skyscrapers, it offers nearly 8km
of watery respite for an estimated
one million visitors each year.
Well-kept public swimming areas,
boat rental outfits, a sailing school,
waterfront restaurants and private
cabanas line the shore. "When the
weather's good we come here,"
says media consultant Ralf Strobl,
who's known to sleep in his cabana
in a marina near the U1 stop. To
really experience life like a Viennese,
this is a must-visit.
alte-donau.info

Lake life
——
Less than 50km from Vienna,
Lake Neusiedl is Austria's
largest lake. Protected
by Unesco, it is home to
hundreds of rare birds and is a
favourite spot for windsurfers,
kayakers and swimmers. Take
the train from Hauptbahnhof to
Neusiedl am See for an easy
summer day trip.

Alte Donau activities

01 Swimming: The water
is clean and easily
accessible from most parts
of the riverbank, especially
those within reach of the
U1 stop – just be careful
near some of the rocky
edges. There's an
outdoor pool at 91
Arbeiterstrandbadstrasse,
1220 too.

02 Sailing: Alte Donau offers
rentals of sailing vessels at
Segelschule Hofbauer
(*hofbauer.at*) on the river's
eastern bank.

03 Rowing: Pedal, rowing and
electric boats (no motors
here, thanks) are also
available for hire for the
more leisurely watertrip.
Again, Segelschule
Hofbauer is your best bet.

Cycling
Pedal of honour

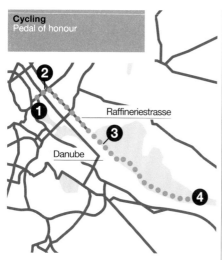

Raffineriestrasse

Danube

Running routes
Jog on

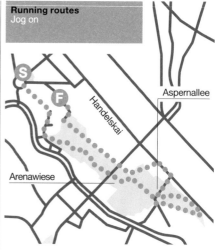

Aspernallee

Handelskai

Arenawiese

While most people arrive in Vienna by air or train there's the odd zealot who pedals into town via the 390km Danube Cycle Path. This paved trail crosses national borders from the banks of Passau to the old town of Bratislava. It's quite a simple ride affording views of the region's most scenic spots including picturesque villages, orchards and the odd vineyard – a welcome sight after a day in the saddle. And while we won't insist you ride the whole trail, we'd recommend venturing out for a half-day's cycle just beyond the city limits.

Danube trail
Follow the great river out of town

STARTING POINT: Leopoldstadt
DISTANCE: 21km

Start by hiring a bike from ❶ *Pedal Power* in Leopoldstadt: the company has been in operation for nearly two decades and will provide you with the best wheels to set off on the Danube trail. Exit the shop and turn right along Venediger Au then right again along the bicycle path of Lassallestrasse. Pedal for a little over five minutes and once you've crossed the Danube via ❷ *Reichsbruecke* bridge you have the option to follow the Danube cycle path upstream toward Wachau or south towards Bratislava. We recommend heading downstream to ride through the lush greenery of ❸ *Lobau*. This water forest is home to around 100 different brooding bird species, including the kingfisher, ringed plover and grey heron. You'll soon hit the less-than-charming tank farm for OMV Tanklager. But the path continues and views do improve as you reach ❹ *Donau-Auen National Park*. Once here you can break from the peloton and head back upstream into town. That evening's *spritzwein* will have been well and truly earned.

①
The Green Prater
Get in touch with nature

DISTANCE: 13km
GRADIENT: Flat
DIFFICULTY: Easy
HIGHLIGHT: Lusthaus, a 16th-century hunting lodge built by Emperor Maximillian II, is a picturesque restaurant to enjoy the best of Viennese cuisine
BEST TIME: Any weekday during daylight hours
NEAREST STATION: Praterstern

The Prater is a former imperial hunting ground and is one of the most liked parks in the city, covering an area of 6 sq km. Even though it's located just a few kilometres from Stephansplatz, the landscape is wholly natural with vast lawns, woods and streams. The park also has its own hiking route known officially as City Hiking Trail 9.

Start at Praterstern Station and head down Hauptallee through towering trees on either side, passing the Pratermuseum. Take a right when you reach the Jantschweg onto an unpaved path among the soaring trees, turning left and running straight on.

As it has no set route, you've got the freedom to move around as you wish, passing the Konstantinteich along the way, over a bridge past the clay tennis courts of the Wiener Park Club and back into the woods along the Lusthausstrasse.

Further down you'll reach Hauptalle; make a right and continue until you arrive at Lusthaus at the centre of a roundabout. To make your way back up, circle around the Lusthauswasser next to the Golf-Club Wien. Cross the main road of Aspernallee until you end up next to the Wirtschaftsuniversitat Wien to walk back up, weaving your way north to Praterstern Station.

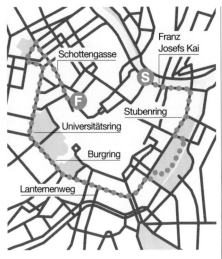

Ringstrasse
Seeing the sights as you run

DISTANCE: 5km
GRADIENT: Some small hills
DIFFICULTY: Easy
HIGHLIGHT: Getting to see all of Vienna's best
monuments on a single route
BEST TIME: Weekdays, otherwise you may have to dodge
a few tourists
NEAREST STATION: Schwedenplatz

Dating back from 1858, Ringstrasse is a handsome collection of – deep breath – neoclassical, neo-gothic, neo-renaissance and neo-Baroque monuments.

The best place to start is Marienbrucke near Schwedenplatz. Run anti-clockwise along Franz-Josefs-Kai to Urania, the public-educational institute and observatory. Here you can turn onto the Sightseeing Bicycle Path Ringstrasse, which will give you a clearer path to follow and ensure you don't miss any sites along the way. On your right you pass Otto Wagner's Postparkasse, leading you into the Vienna City Park where you'll see the golden Johann Strauss II monument. Exit the park past the Vienna State Opera in the Karlsplatz before ending up at the imposing Imperial Palace. The Museum of Fine Arts is just across the street, while the Museumsquartier is just behind. Mark it down for a visit later.

Go past the Burggarten and Volksgarten on your right to find the parliament, city hall, Burgtheater and University of Vienna – all fine examples of art deco architecture. Next to Schottentor Station across from the university is the neo-gothic Votivkirche.

The path will now slope slightly downward, making it a little easier to make your way toward the Donaukanal past the Vienna Stock Exchange on your right.

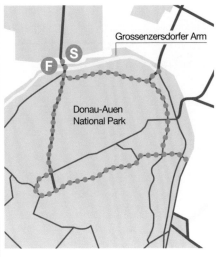

Beaver Run Circular Trail, Donau-Auen National Park
Into the wild

DISTANCE: 6km
GRADIENT: Flat
DIFFICULTY: Medium
HIGHLIGHT: The chance to see beavers at work
BEST TIME: Early morning or late afternoon
NEAREST STATIONS: J99B to Kaposigasse or 26A to
Gross-Enzersdorf

Swap the city for a run through the verdant Donau-Auen National Park, which stretches all the way from Vienna to Bratislava. The blue Danube snakes its way through this protected park; its inhabitants include the crafty beaver, that, if you're lucky, you'll encounter on your jog.

The best place to begin is at Esslinger Furt. As you enter the park you'll find yourself surrounded by acorn trees and shrubs on a trail that crosses open terrain, meadows and fields. Keep your eyes peeled for beaver tracks. Take a breather when you reach the forester's lodge. Here you'll find the beaver corral, so slow down and catch a glimpse of the furry fellows; your chances are best in the late afternoon or at dusk. Continue along the Vorwerkstrasse in the direction of Gross-Enzersdorf. Follow the running route as it turns left just before the Kasernbrückerl Bridge. From here you can follow the trail bordering the forest until you're back at the Esslinger Furt.

Where to buy
—

Top spots for sportswear in the capital:
Bach Sport (*bachsport.at*) in Wieden, Bogner
(*bogner.com*) in Innere Stadt for all-weather gear
and Tony's Laufshop (*tonys-laufshop.at*) for trainers.

Walks
Find your own Vienna

Vienna is a city best explored on foot: its many districts are modest in size but into each are packed centuries' worth of architectural styles and historic sites. A brisk walk, for instance, between two of the city's most famous buildings, St Stephen's Cathedral and the Neue Burg palace, takes about 10 minutes but you'll want to savour the many other landmarks, shops and cafés – and it could take all day. So fortify yourself with a hearty breakfast and join us on our favourite strolls through Vienna.

NEIGHBOURHOOD 01

Josefstadt to Neubau
Mix it up

Up until the late 19th century Vienna's 8th district, Josefstadt, was a military exercise and parade ground. It may be the city's smallest district with the least number of green spaces but what it lacks in size and foliage it more than makes up for in cultural attractions and venerable ex-residents. Painter Gustav Klimt, Nobel Prize-winning zoologist Karl von Frisch and writer Marie von Ebner-Eschenbach all called Josefstadt home, while noble families chose this district for their summer palaces, four of which remain. It's also where you will find one of the city's oldest theatres: Theater in der Josefstadt.

Neighbouring Neubau (the 7th district), which begins at Lerchenfelder Strasse, is a much older area; it was first settled in the 12th century. The district has long been favoured by tradespeople and today it teems with designer shops, independent boutiques, small artisanal coffeehouses and gastropubs. But it is not impervious to the mainstream: Mariahilferstrasse to the south is Vienna's biggest and busiest shopping stretch, bordered by a train station at one end and Museumsquartier at the other. The area is also home to several co-working spaces for creatives.

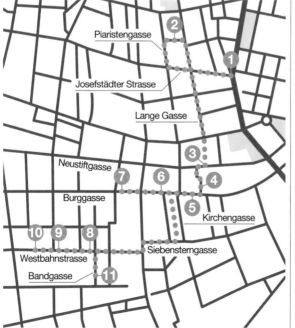

Caffeine hit
Josefstadt to Neubau walk

Start with a morning *melange*, soaking up the traditional atmosphere of ❶ *Café Eiles* at the foot of the main thoroughfare Josefstädter Strasse. Once sufficiently caffeinated, head up the hill, taking a right on Lange Gasse before turning left onto Maria-Treu-Gasse, a cosy side street that leads to the stunning 18th-century Piarist church. Stop for a wholesome crêpe breakfast at ❷ *Café der Provinz*.

Getting there

The number 2 tram will drop you on Josefstädter Strasse (Rathaus Station) where this tour starts. Another option is to travel via subway on Line U2 of the U-Bahn to Rathaus Station. Walk south a block to reach the beginning of the route.

Stroll back to Josefstädter Strasse via Piaristengasse before turning left past the illustrious Theater in der Josefstadt. Next, take a right turn onto Lange Gasse, formerly the main street of the district and one of the longest (hence the name). Take note of the structures on both sides: Lange Gasse has a bit of everything – Baroque buildings, ponderous imperial 19th-century blocks and lightweight Jugendstil tenement houses. Once you reach the end of the street, cross the road and duck into one of the many *durchgänge* (passageways – see page 120) that slice through typical Viennese apartment blocks.

You'll emerge on Neustiftgasse. Cross the street and indulge in some organic vegan ice cream at ❸ *Veganista* (worth it whatever your dietary requirements). Exit to your left and take Sankt-Ulrichs-Platz alleyway leading onto Ulrichsplatz, a Baroque ensemble of extremely well-preserved burgher housing presided over by the eponymous church.

On the opposite side, the square is bordered by Burggasse, a time-tested hip stretch with a number of shopping spots and bars. But before you leave Ulrichsplatz, ❹ *Ulrich* on the east side of the church is a top pick for both lunch and dinner. If you are in the mood for some vintage clothes shopping, check out ❺ *Burggasse24* just across the square. The street bursts into life in the evening and both the 1950s-style ❻ *Espresso* and more modern ❼ *Wirr* further along are good choices for a coffee or late-afternoon drink.

Head back east along Burggasse and cut into another *durchgänge*

at number 51, Adlerhof. Once you work your way out you will find yourself facing a small square at Siebensterngasse. Look up at the building on its western edge that dominates the block – it's a fine example of a grand Viennese corner house. Make a right and follow the tram tracks onto Westbahnstrasse. Hop in to ❽ *Zàmm*, a venue that models itself on Oscar Wilde's famous phrase, "With freedom, books, flowers and the moon, who could not be happy?" and sells all manner of fashionable magazines.

Once you've had your fill of independent publishing (and more coffee), browse some of the finest mid-century Scandinavian design at ❾ *Designqvist* further up the street. To finish things off in style, continue along to the legendary ❿ *WestLicht* photography museum, which is sure to have a thought-provoking exhibition on. Afterwards, walk back along Westbahnstrasse and take a right onto Bandgasse to ⓫ *Hotel am Brillantengrund* for a relaxing drink followed by a Filipino or Mediterranean-style meal.

NEIGHBOURHOOD 02

Freihausviertel
All about art

The Freihausviertel is a portion of Vienna's 4th district that hugs the famous Naschmarkt food market and spreads out towards Wiedner Hauptstrasse. It has morphed from a destitute, dingy, almost-forgotten zone to a small but lively cultural hub packed with art, design, shopping and delicious things to eat and drink.

In the 1700s this was where Vienna's less-salubrious population made things; many guilds were based here, and artists have always been attracted to the area's easygoing and creative atmosphere (Mozart's *The Magic Flute* premiered in a theatre around here). However, after the destruction that resulted from the Second World War the area fell into slow decline.

At around the same time that the Naschmarkt was updated and rejuvenated in the 1990s, art dealer Georg Kargl and some colleagues formed a neighbourhood association and opened businesses here. Kargl's main gallery opened on Schleifmühlgasse in 1998, and the street has been a vibrant artery ever since – it's now home to a cluster of high-end contemporary galleries. Interesting small-scale boutiques, restaurants and cafés complete the scene. This part of the Freihausviertel is once again a place where the Viennese make and show things, as well as enjoy them at their own pace.

Creative enclave
Freihausviertel walk

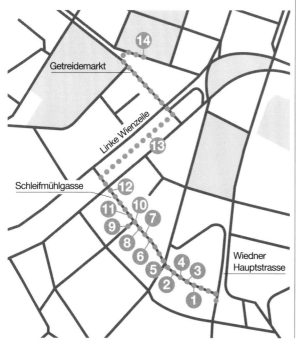

This walk starts where Wiedner Hauptstrasse and Schleifmühlgasse meet. Jump straight into some art appreciation at ❶ *Gabriele Senn Galerie*, an airy space filled with conceptual work by artists including Cosima von Bonin and Claire Fontaine, and photographer Elfie Semotan (Austria's answer to Annie Leibovitz). Neighbouring Christine König Galerie, an arts-industry veteran, exhibits edgy works by big names such as Ai Weiwei and cheeky Romanian-Slovak duo Anetta Mona Chisa and Lucia Tkacova, while next door Kerstin Engholm Galerie shows work from the top artists of 1990s central Europe and beyond.

Then comes Schleifmühlgasse's anchor: Georg Kargl's 350 sq m main space ❷ *Georg Kargl Fine Arts*. The gallery boasts three levels and multiple rooms. Work by Austrian painter duo Muntean/Rosenblum or photographers Clegg & Guttmann is often on view here. Kargl's adjacent Box space has a strong architectural concept (note the slanted mirrors in the façade) by artist Richard Artschwager and local architecture firm Jabornegg & Pálffy.

Across the street is less art and more commerce: luxurious, high-ceilinged flower shop ❸ *Blumenkraft* was designed by architect Gregor Eichinger; owner Christine Fink is a master of unusual and beautiful flower arrangements. Next door, fashion designer Jutta Pregenzer runs a shop called ❹ *Pregenzer*, with her own designs (created in her adjacent apartment) along with Maison Margiela, Essentiel Antwerp and more. If you are in the mood for more contemporary art, head upstairs to ❺ *Galerie Andreas Huber*.

Cross Margaretengasse and the scene shifts from art and design to shopping: to the left are design shops ❻ *Rauminhalt* and ❼ *Mood*. The former offers exquisite furniture pieces spanning the modern and contemporary eras; the latter offers more recent greats from brands such as Vitra and Tom Dixon. A few steps away is ❽ *Flo Vintage*, one of the nation's best vintage clothing shops, tracing 100 years of fashion history. Here you'll also find another exhibition space belonging to Kargl, Permanent, which allows artists to mount longer-term exhibitions. On the corner, cookbook shop ❾ *Babette's* offers some 2,500 recipe books and cooking courses (it is named after the film *Babette's Feast*).

By now you'll no doubt be ready for some sustenance. Across the street is ❿ *Vollpension*, an "intergenerational" retro café where grandmas bake and serve what are widely touted as the city's best cakes. On the next corner, across Mühlgasse, is ⓫ *Café Anzengruber*,

Getting there

Line U1 on the U-Bahn will bring you to Taubstummengasse Station; exit and walk north, taking the third street on your left and then the second street on your right to reach the starting point. Another option is to walk south from Karlsplatz Station along Wiedner Hauptstrasse.

a traditional *beisl* complete with marble tables, Thonet chairs and a slightly rundown interior that attracts creatives after 16.00. For a slightly more subdued coffeehouse experience continue to the cosy, vaulted ceilinged ⓬ *Café Amacord* on the right, or save your hunger for the ⓭ *Naschmarkt* (Vienna's legendary food market) just across the Rechte Wienzeile. There are eating spots and food stands aplenty, selling fruit, fish, spices and locally made Gegenbauer vinegar (*see page 57*).

Exit at the far end of the market, admiring the art nouveau exterior of the Secession building (*see page 99*) opposite. Turn left down Getreidemarkt and take a right to end your tour with a final dose of art, this time from the Old Masters. The 1877 Akademie der bildenden Künste Wien building is a marvel, dating to Austria's imperial period. Head to the ⓮ *Gemäldegalerie*, where you'll find works by Rembrandt, Cranach and Rubens, and the ultimate Hieronymus Bosch: "The Last Judgment".

Address book

01 Gabriele Senn Galerie
   1A Schleifmühlgasse, 1040
   +43 (0)1 585 2580
   galeriesenn.at

02 Georg Kargl Fine Arts
   5 Schleifmühlgasse, 1040
   +43 (0)1 585 4199
   georgkargl.com

03 Blumenkraft
   4 Schleifmühlgasse, 1040
   +43 (0)1 585 7727
   blumenkraft.at

04 Pregenzer
   4 Schleifmühlgasse, 1040
   +43 (0)1 586 5758
   pregenzer.com

05 Galerie Andreas Huber
   6-8 Schleifmühlgasse, 1040
   +43 (0)1 586 0237
   galerieandreashuber.at

06 Rauminhalt
   13 Schleifmühlgasse, 1040
   +43 650 409 9892
   rauminhalt.at

07 Mood
   13 Schleifmühlgasse, 1040
   +43 (0)1 236 3131
   moodwien.at

08 Flo Vintage
   15A Schleifmühlgasse, 1040
   +43 (0)1 586 0773
   flovintage.com

09 Babette's
   17 Schleifmühlgasse, 1040
   +43 (0)1 585 5165
   babettes.at

10 Vollpension
   16 Schleifmühlgasse, 1040
   +43 (0)1 585 0464
   vollpension.wien

11 Café Anzengruber
   19 Schleifmühlgasse, 1040
   +43 (0)1 587 8297

12 Café Amacord
   15 Rechte Wienzeile, 1040
   +43 (0)1 587 4709
   amacord-cafe.at

13 Naschmarkt
   Along Rechte and 1060
   wienernaschmarkt.eu

14 Gemäldegalerie
   Schillerplatz 3, 1010
   +43 (0)1 588 162 222
   akademiegalerie.at

NEIGHBOURHOOD 03
Leopoldstadt
Heritage and culture

Vienna's 2nd district, known as Leopoldstadt after an Austrian emperor of yore, has always been a contrast to the 1st. Historically it was waltz to the 1st's opera, offering populist rather than highbrow culture. Before the Second World War, Leopoldstadt bustled with busy theatres, coffeehouses and street life, which reflected the population – for 300 years its large Jewish community lent it the nickname Matzo Island.

That war decimated much of Viennese and Jewish life too. Leopoldstadt remained dark and dusty until well into the 2000s but is now highly regarded – in 2008 the U2 subway line was extended and more artists and young entrepreneurs arrived. Since 2010 a glittering beacon has sat at the district's tip: French architect Jean Nouvel's glass-façaded Sofitel hotel and Stilwerk design complex. The Jewish community is back too and it's not unusual to see Orthodox Jews alongside young creatives.

Near iconic Prater park, the architecturally interesting University of Economics and Business campus opened in 2013 and the upcoming Nordbahnhof urban-renewal project will anchor a new neighbourhood by 2025. And Praterstrasse, the once-grand thoroughfare, is reclaiming its former power with new cafés and innovative shops. In many ways this walk slices through layers of history and parallel cultures to explore Vienna's other side.

A little bit of everything
Leopoldstadt walk

Start at the southeastern tip of Augarten park in front of MuTh (the theatre hall for Vienna Boys' Choir – *see page 102*) and the recently renovated ❶ *Filmarchiv Austria*. Vienna's film archive has housed a mediatheque, shop and study centre since 1997 in the former cook's quarters and stables of the Palais Augarten and is well worth a look.

Walk along Obere Augartenstrasse toward the imposing Fläkturme (a bunker tower) at the edge of the park, one of six apparently indestructible structures built by the Nazis to defend the city from air raids in the Second World War. To your right is a gate to the ❷ *Wiener Porzellanmanufaktur Augarten*, a porcelain factory with a museum and shop. After perusing (and perhaps buying) the wares, double back toward the subway stop; cross the street and enter Grosse Sperlgasse.

Walk three blocks to Haidgasse and turn right. At the end of the street you will find ❸ *Karmelitermarkt*, which has been an open marketplace since 1671. Stands from farmers and a multicultural crowd fill the market on Fridays and Saturdays, while permanent stands and restaurant spaces are open the rest of the week. Some of our top picks include Cafemima (stand 21-24) for breakfast, Kaas am Markt (stand 33-36) for Austrian specialities such as marmalade and pumpkin-seed oil, and Tewa (stand 26-32) for excellent regional wines and various cuisines.

After exiting the market, walk south on Hollandstrasse until you reach Kleine Sperlgasse. Turn left

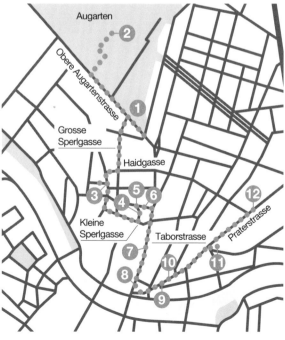

and carry on to Karmeliterplatz, a square named after the Carmelite monks who settled here in the 1600s. Here ❹ *Wundertüte* boutique sells gifts, jewellery and women's clothes, and ❺ *Schank zum Reichsapfel* serves Austrian wine with specialities such as beef goulash and *apfelstrudel* in a wood-lined dining room (and at tables outdoors in summer). Don't leave the square without entering the Baroque jewel, ❻ *St Josef Church*.

Turn right onto Taborstrasse and walk one block south to the imposing ❼ *Produktenbörse*. It was once a commodity exchange and the interior vaulting is visible in the organic food shop on its ground floor. More impressive is the part where agricultural goods were once traded; it's now the site of Odeon Theater. Once back outside, walk south towards the two tall buildings at the end of the street by the canal: on the left is Nouvel's Sofitel Vienna Stephansdom (at night the hotel lights up with artworks by Pipilotti Rist) and ❽ *Stilwerk*, a design mall with stores such as BoConcept and Edition Werbach. Note the hotel's slanted roof: its pattern mirrors the

tiling on St Stephen's Cathedral, visible across the canal.

Exit Stilwerk onto Praterstrasse. Cross Grosse Mohrengasse and stop at Song for avant garde fashion (*see page 64*). You can also admire the contemporary art at ❾ *Projektraum Viktor Bucher* or pause at ❿ *Café Ansari (see page 36)*, designed by Gregor Eichinger as a "coffeehouse for the future".

Continue on to Tempelgasse and turn right, then immediately left onto Czerningasse. You'll see ⓫ *Theater Nestroyhof Hamakom*, which offers performances and concerts in a historical space that was reclaimed in 2008, its foyer having been used as a supermarket. The venue is an example of the rediscovery of the neighbourhood's cultural legacy.

To finish with a dose of period furniture and musical instruments, head back to Praterstrasse and walk north until you hit Afrikanergasse. Turn let and carry on to the ⓬ *Johann Strauss Apartment*, where the composer lived and wrote Austria's unofficial national anthem "The Blue Danube" waltz in 1867.

Getting there

Take Line U2 of the U-Bahn to Taborstrasse station. The Augarten exit will take you to the park's southeastern point, where the walk begins. The 2nd district is just across the Donaukanal from the 1st district so it is also easily accessible on foot.

Address book

01 Filmarchiv Austria
1E Obere Augartenstrasse, 1020
+43 (0)1 216 1300
filmarchiv.at

02 Wiener Porzellanmanufaktur Augarten
1 Obere Augartenstrasse, 1020
+43 (0)1 2112 4200
augarten.at

03 Karmelitermarkt
Intersection of Leopoldsgasse and Haidgasse, 1020

04 Wundertüte
2 Karmeliterplatz, 1020
+43 664 283 5546
wundertuete.at

05 Schank zum Reichsapfel
3 Karmeliterplatz, 1020
+43 (0)1 212 2579
zumreichsapfel.at

06 St Josef Church
10 Karmelitergasse, 1020

07 Produktenbörse
10 Taborstrasse, 1020
boersewien.at

08 Stilwerk
1 Praterstrasse, 1020
+43 664 8873 0475
stilwerk.de/wien

09 Projektraum Viktor Bucher
13/1 Praterstrasse, 1020
+43 (0)1 212 6930
projektraum.at

10 Café Ansari
15 Praterstrass, 1020
+43 (0)1 276 5102
cafeansari.at

11 Theater Nestroyhof Hamakom
1 Nestroyplatz, 1020
+43 (0)1 8900 314
hamakom.at

12 Johann Strauss Apartment
5 Afrikanergasse, 1020
+43 (0)1 214 0121
wienmuseum.at

NEIGHBOURHOOD 04
Wieden
Architectural grandeur

The city's 3rd district, which lies to the southeast of the city centre, is picturesquely framed by the canal to the east and the landscaped greenery of the Unesco World Heritage listed, French-style Belvederegarten to the west. Here you will find the Belvedere complex with its two Baroque palaces, now showcasing a remarkable collection of art from the medieval period to the 20th century, and further south, the contemporary art space 21er Haus (*see page 98*). The district is also home to the eccentric, organic forms of the Hundertwasserhaus – designed by Austrian artist Friedensreich Hundertwasser (*see page 73*) and overseen by architects Josef Krawina and Peter Pelikan – and the bakery-bistro Joseph Brot vom Pheinsten (*see page 45*) that arguably serves the best apple torte in town.

The neighbouring 4th district of Wieden, which extends south from Karlsplatz, is Vienna's oldest suburb. After the Second World War it belonged to the Soviet sector for a decade. Today this is where you'll find the bustling Café Goldegg as well as The Heroes' Monument of the Red Army. At the district's northern tip lies the historic Karlsplatz (its namesake St Charles's Church was built in 1715) and the nearby Wien Museum. This area is also known as the city's diplomatic quarter as it's peppered with embassies from around the globe.

Building an empire
Wieden walk

Begin your day in the 4th district at the corner of Argentinierstrasse and Goldeggasse, with a morning meal at ❶ *Café Goldegg*. This friendly coffeehouse and art nouveau gem serves classics such as sausages and *semmel* (Viennese bread) and has a particularly popular breakfast menu. Once you've had your fill, step outside and continue east along Goldeggasse until you reach Prinz Eugen-Strasse.

Turn left and walk along the side of the Belvederegarten until you see the ❷ *Upper Belvedere*. Its two palaces are exquisite examples of 1700s Baroque architecture and were designed by Johann Lucas von Hildebrandt. The terraced garden, by French landscape designer Dominique Girard, resembles the royal park he built at Versailles. Once the summer residence of Prince Eugene of Savoy, the palaces have been repurposed as museums of Austrian art.

If you only have time for one painting make it Gustav Klimt's "The Kiss" in the Upper Belvedere. This example of Vienna's Secession movement was painted in 1907-1908 at the height of Klimt's Golden Phase. Once you have wandered the palace's high-ceilinged marble halls – where the Austrian State Treaty was signed in 1955, ending the country's occupation by the four Allied powers after the Second World War – cross the gravel paths to the Lower Belvedere and enjoy the view over Vienna.

Exit the park and turn left onto Rennweg. Follow the road to see Austro-Hungarian architect Otto

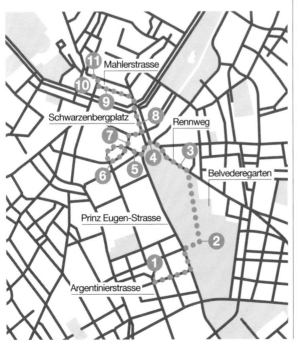

Getting there
———
Take the S-Bahn or the U-Bahn line U1 to the 4th district's Hauptbahnhof Wien Station and walk to Goldeggasse from there. Otherwise you can use the tram and walk several blocks from Schloss Belvedere tram stop.

Address book

01 Café Goldegg
    49 Argentinierstrasse, 1040
    +43 (0)1 505 9162
    cafegoldegg.at
02 Upper Belvedere
    27 Prinz Eugen-Strasse,
    1030
    +43 (0)1 7955 7134
    belvedere.at
03 Palais Hoyos
    5 Rennweg, 1030
04 Heroes' Monument
    of the Red Army
    Schwarzenbergplatz, 1040
05 French embassy
    2 Technikerstrasse, 1040
06 St Charles's Church
    1 Kreuzherrengasse, 1040
    +43 (0)1 504 6187
    karlskirche.at
07 Wien Museum
    8 Karlsplatz, 1040
    +43 (0)1 505 8747
    wienmuseum.at
08 Zum Scharfen Rene
    15 Schwarzenbergplatz,
    1010
    +43 (0) 699 1799 9888
    rkachlir.wix.com/
    zumscharfenrene
09 Petkov
    5 Mahlerstrasse, 1010
    +43 (0)1 513 6480
    petkov.at
10 Vienna State Opera
    2 Opernring, 1010
    +43 (0)1 514 442 250
    wiener-staatsoper.at
11 Sacher Eck
    38 Kärntner Strasse, 1010
    +43 (0)1 5145 6699
    sacher.com

Wagner's neo-renaissance ③ *Palais Hoyos*, built in 1891, before continuing on your way to Schwarzenbergplatz. Here you'll find the ④ *Heroes' Monument of the Red Army*, a Second World War memorial to Soviet soldiers who helped defeat the Nazis in Austria. Pass the fountain and cross the street to get to the grand ⑤ *French embassy* on Technikerstrasse. Continue down the road to reach Mattiellistrasse, where you'll see the embassies of Australia and New Zealand.

You can't miss the 72-metre-high dome of ⑥ *St Charles's Church*, a monumental Baroque example dating from 1715. The church, designed by architect Johann Bernard Fischer von Erlach, was commissioned by Emperor Charles VI to mark the end of an outbreak of the plague and features world-renowned frescoes by Johann Michael Rottmayr.

Walk across Karlsplatz, past the Tilgner Brunnen fountain and enter the ⑦ *Wien Museum* (*see page 93*) housed in a building by Oswald

Haerdtl, to brush up on your history all the way from the Neolithic Age to the mid-20th century (admission is free on the first Sunday of every month).

Once you've learned about Vienna's rich past and explored designs by Adolf Loos and works by Egon Schiele, head east along Lothringerstrasse and make a left back onto Schwarzenbergplatz, at the corner of which is ⑧ *Zum Scharfen Rene*, a family-run Viennese food stand which serves the famous *käsekrainer* (sausage) named after a region of the former Austrian empire.

Keep going until you find yourself at the 1st district's Kärntner Ring, and continue to Schwarzenbergstrasse. Take a left at Mahlerstrasse and be sure to peer into the small 1905-founded family cobbler ⑨ *Petkov*. Finally, head west to ⑩ *Vienna State Opera*, which first opened with a performance of Mozart's *Don Giovanni* in 1869, and finish at ⑪ *Sacher Eck* opposite with a slice of sweet temptation: the original chocolate *sachertorte*.

NEIGHBOURHOOD 05
Innere Stadt
Mighty monuments

No trip to Vienna is complete without a thorough exploration of the
1st district – the historic heart of the city. Until the walls encircling
it were demolished in the 19th century, everything beyond was
considered outside the municipality. Even today these outer
districts are still referred to as *vorstädte* (suburbs). The Ringstrasse
– opened by Emperor Franz Joseph in 1865 to much fanfare – now
follows the path of the old city walls, and this is where you will find
some of Vienna's most renowned tourist attractions, from Baroque
palaces to impossibly elaborate churches.

Consider yourself warned: the delights of the 1st district are
no secret. Be prepared to share them with hordes of enthusiastic
sightseers (many of whom will never venture beyond the Innere
Stadt). Luckily Vienna's big hits are many – few cities can boast
architectural riches as abundant as those in the Austrian capital,
meaning that the throngs of tourists are diluted somewhat. You
will find that weekdays are marginally less busy and will give you
a more authentic taste of everyday Vienna.

Take a leaf out of the locals' book and slow your pace down a
notch or two: take time to observe the storekeepers quietly setting
up shop for the day or the suit-sporting pen-pushers enjoying a
leisurely lunch, and you will find that this is a city best enjoyed
at a relaxed tempo. Those palaces aren't going anywhere.

Vienna's powerhouse
Innere Stadt walk

Start your walk at the steps of the
❶ *Austrian Parliament Building*
on Doktor-Karl-Renner-Ring. The
5.5-metre-high statue of goddess
Athena that stands guard over the
Greek revival building was chosen
by architect Theophil Hansen as
a symbol of wisdom, strategy, war
and peace. Head south across
Schmerlingplatz to pay a visit to
the ❷ *Justizpalast*. The doors to
this grandiose neo-renaissance
building opened in 1881 but a violent
protest in 1927 sparked a fire that
destroyed its Supreme Court and
library. The courts were relocated
temporarily until the building
reopened in the 1930s.

Turn right out of the building and
head straight toward the Museum of
Natural History, then right to make a
pit stop at the ❸ *Museumsquartier* (*see
page 96*). This is one of the largest
cultural precincts in the world and it
houses about 70 facilities, including
the Architekturzentrum Wien and
Leopold Museum. After wandering
through your pick of the museum and
gallery halls (tickets are available), exit
past the Q21 creative workspace and
cross Museumsplatz to meander
through the perfectly tended gardens
of Maria-Theresien-Platz. Exit at the
other side and head across the road
to pass the outer castle gates of
❹ *Äusseres Burgtor* and the
Heldenplatz (Heroes' Square).
Through the gate you will spot a
monument of two riders, portraying
Archduke Charles and Prince
Eugene of Savoy facing each other.
Head back out of the gates and
loop down around Neue Burg to
enter Burggarten.

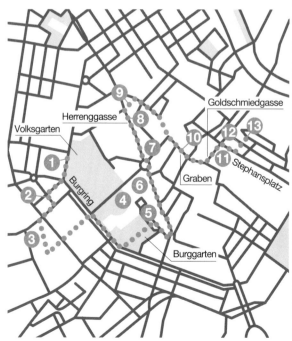

Address book

01	Austrian Parliament Building
	3 Doktor-Karl-Renner-Ring, 1010
	+43 (0)1 401 100
	parlament.gv.at
02	Justizpalast
	11 Schmerlingplatz, 1010
	+43 (0)1 521 520
	ogh.gv.at
03	Museumsquartier
	1 Museumsplatz, 1070
	+43 (0)1 523 5881
	mqw.at
04	Äusseres Burgtor
	Heldenplatz, 1010
05	Palmenhaus
	1 Burggarten, 1010
	+43 (0)1 533 1033
	palmenhaus.at
06	Hofburg Palace
	Michaelerkuppel, 1010
	+43 (0)1 533 7570
	hofburg-wien.at
07	Looshaus building
	3 Michaelerplatz, 1010
08	Palais Ferstel
	4 Strauchgasse, 1010
	+43 (0)1 533 3763
	palaisevents.at
09	Ferstel Passage
	16 Herrengasse, 1010
	ferstel-passage.at
10	Pestsäule
	Graben, 1010
11	St Stephen's Cathedral
	3 Stephansplatz, 1010
	+43 (0)1 515 523 054
	stephanskirche.at
12	Schönbichler
	4 Wollzeile, 1010
	+43 (0)1 512 1816
13	Figlmüller
	5 Wollzeile, 1010
	+43 (0)1 512 6177
	figlmueller.at

Getting there

Hotels within the 1st district are a short walk or taxi ride from the starting point. The nearest U-Bahn station is Volkstheater and lines U2 and U3 service it. Alternatively, trams stop at Doktor-Karl-Renner-Ring and Stadiongasse/Parliament.

Enter through the second gate and walk past the city's monument to Mozart and towards ⑤ *Palmenhaus*. This ornate greenhouse was built in 1822 and then renovated in 1901 but again fell into disrepair in the 1980s. After a major refurbishment the building was reopened in the late 1990s as a restaurant and bar – this is a good spot to enjoy some lunch. After a break, circle around the Albertina Museum and continue onto Josefsplatz, passing beneath the belly of the Spanish Riding School. This building is one of many making up the Baroque ⑥ *Hofburg Palace*. If you have time, see the famous Lipizzaner horses at the riding school and the Sisi Museum.

Exit back onto the Romanesque piazza of Michaelerplatz and head north past the modernist ⑦ *Looshaus building* (*see page 111*) and along Herrengasse until you reach ⑧ *Palais Ferstel.* At the junction veer left up Herrengasse and on your right you will see the entrance to ⑨ *Ferstel Passage*. Both passage and palace were designed by architect Heinrich von Ferstel for the Austro-Hungarian National Bank and the

Vienna Stock Exchange in 1860. The ornamented passageway is now a luxury shopping destination – look for the excellent chocolatier Xocolat. At the end turn right onto Freyung and walk down the pedestrianised streets until you reach Graben, the city's well-heeled shopping strip. Shortly after you pass St Peter's Catholic Church you'll see ⑩ *Pestsäule*, or the Holy Trinity column, built in 1679 after one of Vienna's last big plague epidemics.

Head left via Goldschmiedgasse past the horse-drawn carriages and turn right onto Stephansplatz. This will be a welcome change from oversized shops: much smaller, quintessentially Austrian brands line the left side of the road. Once you pass ⑪ *St Stephen's Cathedral* (*see page 111*), across the road to your left will be a narrow passageway marked with two large wooden doors. At the end of the passageway is the historical retailer ⑫ *Schönbichler*, which sells a variety of natural teas. Cross the road into a second passageway and walk down to the world-renowned ⑬ *Figlmüller* restaurant. Step inside for a succulent wiener schnitzel.

Resources
—— Inside
knowledge

You've taken in Vienna's imperial beauty, its multifaceted cultural scene, its delectable wines and comforting cuisine. But how to connect it all? Our guide to getting around will have you feeling at home in no time, from easing into the public transit system to conversing Wiener-style.

We will also provide you with a varied soundtrack to the city to help you get into a Vienna mood; then there's a calendar of unmissable annual events and a selection of the best places at which to spend your time in both fair and foul weather. Either way, don't worry: the Austrian capital is a place where there's always something wonderful to see or do, inside or out.

Transport
Get around town

01 Subway: Vienna's subway system (U-Bahn) and suburban railway (S-Bahn) offer easy ways to get around the city fast. If you're not in town long enough to use an annual pass, which works out at just €1 a day, consider the well-priced passes that run from 24 hours to a whole week and that include discounts on sightseeing and museums. Single rides are €2.20.
wienerlinien.at

02 Bicycle: Vienna's Citybike programme has 120 stations throughout the city. The first hour is free while up to four hours costs €7. The city is expanding its bike network but some narrower streets have no cycle lanes and it can be tight squeezing through.
citybikewien.at

03 Bus and tram: Some 145 bus and 29 tram routes traverse the city, many using vehicles with ultra low floors. Be aware that bus and tram maps are hard to come by and the numbering system is odd. Just ask.
wienerlinien.at

04 On foot: With grand shopping arteries and a warren of side streets, Vienna's 1st district is easily walkable and most sights in neighbouring districts are little more than a stroll.

05 Taxi and private car hire: Taxi fares start at €3.80 and then cost €1.42 per kilometre. If you prefer a private vehicle, book with Austrian Business Car or DaLimousine.
abc.or.at; dalimousine.com

06 Flights: Vienna International Airport at Schwechat is 16 minutes from the city centre by the City Airport Train (Cat).
viennaaircrafthandling.com

07 Other: Don't be surprised to see Viennese adults using push scooters ("rollers" in Austrian vernacular). Not all streets are wide enough for easy biking and this is a quirky yet popular alternative.

Vocabulary
Local lingo

01 Ach geh: oh, come on
02 Beisl: bistro-style restaurant
03 G'spritzt: with sparkling water
04 Ö: short for Austria
05 Passt: literally, "It fits": OK, excellent or perfect
06 Rechnung; zahlen bitte: the bill; I'd like to pay
07 Servus: all-purpose greeting, less formal than *Grüss Gott*
08 Tschick: cigarette
09 Wiederschauen: goodbye
10 Wurstl: sausage

Vienna playlist
Seven top tunes

A genre-spanning Vienna playlist.

01 Johann Strauss II, 'Blue Danube Waltz': The classic. Grand, familiar and sure to send even the laziest feet into a proper waltz.

02 Georg Danzer, 'Die Leut San Alle Deppert – Ausser Mir': If you can understand the words to "Everyone's Stupid But Me", you'll laugh at the typically Viennese grumpiness. If you can't the tune's still catchy.

03 Ultravox, 'Vienna': An early-1980s synth-pop anthem to the city, with lots of layers and a grand ending.

04 Falco, 'Ganz Wien': Before "Rock Me Amadeus" came Falco's "Ganz Wien", a haunting minimalist ode to the city's 1980s pathos.

05 Kruder + Dorfmeister, 'Jazz Master': This bossa nova cut by locals K+D was a lounge classic in the 1990s and recalls the power that was the era's Vienna electronica.

06 Conchita Wurst, 'Rise Like a Phoenix': The bearded lady from the Austrian countryside won the 2014 Eurovision Song Contest, belting out "Phoenix" like a Broadway star.

07 Wanda, 'Bussi Baby': Vienna indie sensation's guitar-driven anthem from 2015.

Best events
What to see

01 Vienna Ball Season, various venues: For four months Vienna hosts guild and themed balls. Highlights are the New Year's Eve and Opera Balls.
November-February, wien.info

02 Mayfest, Leopoldstadt: Prater park hosts free rock concerts on 1 May.
May, praterwien.com

03 Wiener Festwochen, various venues: A month of films, performances and global interdisciplinary and avant garde cultural events.
May-June, festwochen.at

04 Donauinselfest, Donauinsel: Europe's largest open-air music festival draws about three million people.
June, donauinselfest.at

05 Impulstanz, various venues: A dance festival hosted by the Museumsquartier's Volkstheater, Burgtheater and Schauspielhaus.
July-August, impulstanz.com

06 Weinwandertag, various venues: On one late-September weekend Vienna's vintners offer vineyard-hiking trips, serving wines alfresco.
September, wien.info

07 Vienna Contemporary, Marx Halle: The best art fair in Vienna, with a focus on local as well as eastern European art.
September, viennacontemporary.at

08 Vienna Design Week, various venues: Austria's premier design event integrates exhibitions into the city's existing design scene.
September, viennadesignweek.at

09 Viennale, various venues: Vienna's film festival, founded in 1960, specialises in documentaries, experimental works and short films.
October, viennale.at

10 Vienna Christmas Markets, various venues: The city's seasonal markets sell crafts and mulled wine in scenic venues, such as in front of Schönbrunn Palace.
From mid-November

Rainy days
Weather-proof activities

Vienna can have drizzly spells but thankfully its museums are among the world's best and the city's coffee culture is second to none.

01 Austrian National Library, Josefsplatz: As well as being a beautiful spot to while away an afternoon – its central Prunksaal hall is jaw-dropping – the former imperial library in the Hofburg also houses several intriguing museums that most tourists miss. See how the Austro-Hungarians viewed themselves and the wider world in the Map and Globe Museum, take in the papyrus collection or visit the fun Department of Planned Languages and Esperanto Museum: a space that uses images and audio to trace languages, such as Klingon, that didn't evolve naturally.
onb.ac.at/ev

02 Kunsthistorisches Museum, Innere Stadt: A grand edifice built in the late 1800s to exhibit the Habsburg imperial collections, the KHM is famously packed with world-class renaissance and Flemish paintings that you could spend weeks perusing; there are Egyptian and classical collections too. To beat the crowds and explore the depth of Austrian history spend time in the Kunstkammer, an "encyclopedia of knowledge and natural wonders" at the heart of the collection – a museum within the museum.
khm.at

03 Cosy cafés, Innere Stadt: Vienna's world-famous coffee culture is eminently conducive to sitting inside to read, write or muse on a rainy day. Especially cosy spots are:
Café Hawelka, Innere Stadt
hawelka.at
Café Engländer, Innere Stadt
cafe-engländer.com
Café Korb, Innere Stadt
cafekorb.at
For more cafés see page 37

Sunny days
The great outdoors

Sunny days bring the Viennese out in droves. Join them at a *Schanigarten* (pavement café) or in their favourite activities below.

01 Boating on the Alte Donau, Donaustadt: This lake-like former arm of the Danube is a wonderful swimming area but it's even more fun to rent a paddleboat or sailboat for the day and enjoy the entire Donauinsel (Danube Island) area. Rental companies, most of them family-owned, line the banks near the Alte Donau subway stop (*see page 125*). Bring a picnic and cruise to Gänsehäufel Island or paddle further to the Lobau, which is part of the Donau-Auen National Park.
alte-donau.info

02 Hermannskogel in the Wienerwald (Vienna forest), Döbling: A hike through the Wienerwald, an expansive wooded area near the city limits, is never a bad idea. But for views as breathtaking as your exercise, walk along the highest ridge in the city: the Hermannskogel is 524 metres above sea level. At the top you can climb the 27-metre-tall Habsburgswarte tower.

03 Riesenrad at the Wurstelprater, Leopoldstadt: Prater park has been a favourite spot for Viennese to let their hair down since it opened to the public in the 18th century. Today its amusement park, the Wurstelprater, is home to rides, souvenir sellers and traditional restaurants but it's the Riesenrad that most visitors come for. A ride on the giant ferris wheel that hosted intrigue in the film *The Third Man* and helped tug heartstrings in *Before Sunrise* is a perfect way to see the modern city while soaking up a little old-Vienna atmosphere.
wienerriesenrad.com

About Monocle
—— Step inside

In 2007, Monocle was launched as a monthly magazine briefing on global affairs, business, culture, design and much more. We believed there was a globally minded audience of readers who were hungry for opportunities and experiences beyond their national borders.

Today Monocle is a complete media brand with print, audio and online elements – not to mention our expanding retail network and online business. Besides our London HQ we have seven international bureaux in New York, Toronto, Istanbul, Singapore, Tokyo, Zürich and Hong Kong. We continue to grow and flourish and at our core is the simple belief that there will always be a place for a print brand that is committed to telling fresh stories and sending photographers on assignments. It's also a case of knowing that our success is all down to the readers, advertisers and collaborators who have supported us along the way.

Park life
——
Our HQ abuts Paddington Street Gardens

①

International bureaux
Boots on the ground

We have an HQ in London and call upon firsthand reports from our contributors in more than 35 cities around the world. We also have seven international bureaux. For this travel guide, MONOCLE writers Marie-Sophie Schwarzer and Lara Kunze-Concewitz teamed up with Vienna-based Alexei Korolyov, a regular contributor, and Kimberly Bradley, our Vienna correspondent. They also called on the assistance of writers in the city to ensure we have covered the best food, retail, hospitality and entertainment on offer. The aim is to make you, the reader, feel like a local when you visit.

②

Print
Committed to the page

MONOCLE is published 10 times a year. We have stayed loyal to our belief in quality print with two new seasonal publications: THE FORECAST, packed with key insights into the year ahead, and THE ESCAPIST, our summer travel-minded magazine. To sign up visit *monocle.com/subscribe*. Since 2013 we have also been publishing books, like this one, in partnership with Gestalten.